D0005227

FROM THE BOOK:

"Often in a marriage the two partners may be dealing with each other as child to child...."

"One of the myths concerning women in our society is that they must be all things to all people."

"Although there is an alarming divorce rate in this country, when one contemplates the realities of married life, I think it remarkable that people do as well as they do."

"I think the generation gap is a necessity...."

"The American bride has been the victim of a broad cultural discrimination that has shaped her self-image and negated her personhood."

****

"Patricia Helman has written a lucid and readable book... I can't think of any woman who wouldn't be as interested as I was, from the first page to the last."

Eugenia Price

Free To Be A Woman

Patricia Kennedy Helman

MANOR
BOOKS
INC.

A MANOR BOOK............................1973

Manor Books Inc.
329 Fifth Avenue
New York, New York 10016

301.412
H478f
1971

The author is grateful to the following for permission to use
copyrighted material:

Daedalus for selections from "Reflections on Womanhood"
by Erik H. Erikson, reprinted by permission from *Daedalus*,
Journal of the American Academy of Arts and Sciences, Boston,
Massachusetts, Volume 93, Number 2 (Spring 1964).

E. P. Dutton and J. M. Dent & Sons Ltd. for material from
Immanence by Evelyn Underhill.

Harcourt Brace Jovanovich, Inc., for selections from *A Room
of One's Own* by Virginia Woolf, copyright, 1929, by Harcourt
Brace Jovanovich, Inc.; copyright, 1957 by Leonard Woolf. Reprinted by permission of the publishers, the Literary Estate of
Virginia Woolf and The Hogarth Press Ltd.

Holt, Rinehart and Winston, for lines from "The Death
of the Hired Man" from *The Poetry of Robert Frost,* edited by
Edward Connery Lathem. Copyright 1930, 1939, © 1969 by
Holt, Rinehart and Winston, Inc. Copyright © 1958 by Robert
Frost. Copyright © 1967 by Lesley Frost Ballantine. Reprinted
by permission of Holt, Rinehart and Winston, Inc., the Estate of
Robert Frost, and Jonathan Cape Ltd.

The Macmillan Company for lines from "Solitary," reprinted
with permission of The Macmillan Company from *The Col-
lected Poems of Sara Teasdale.* Copyrighted 1926 by The Macmillan Company, renewed 1954 by Mamie T. Wheless.

W. W. Norton & Company for selections reprinted from *Man's
Search for Himself* by Rollo May, Ph.D., with the permission of
the publisher, W. W. Norton & Company, Inc., New York, N.Y.
Copyright, 1953, by W. W. Norton & Company, Inc. Reprinted
also with the permission of George Allen & Unwin Ltd.

Random House, Inc., for material from *The Second Sex* by
Simone de Beauvoir, copyright 1952 by AAK, Inc., and from
Culture Against Man by Jules Henry, copyright © 1963 by
Random House, Inc.

SCM Press Ltd. for material from *Florence Allshorn: A Biography* by J. H. Oldham.

A. P. Watt & Son for lines by A. P. Herbert.

Library of Congress Catalog Card Number: 78-157599

For *Blair*
A small offering
from a grateful and loving heart.

CONTENTS

INTRODUCTION

The decade just ended saw the gods of science put men on the moon and left us with a variety of social and historical phenomena; rebellious students and the accompanying themes of drugs, dissent and a counter culture, a non-stop war, the militant thrust of black power, and problems of pollution and population that hover over the grim decline of American cities.

Not the least of the social phenomena that we have experienced in the last decade is the rise of the Women's Liberation movement and the subsequent reactions in the press and in private lives to anything that might signal major changes in what seemed unchangeable. The parallel exists again where a great civil rights movement on behalf of the Negro gives rise to another women's rights movement, the first real thrust in this area since the franchise was granted. Simone de Beauvoir in the introduction to *The Second Sex* says, "Enough ink has been spilled in the quarreling over feminism, now practically over, and perhaps we should say no more about it."[1] Alas, she was wrong. The ink is flowing again.

Betty Friedan, true to her message in *The Feminine Mystique*, is the power behind NOW (New Organization for Women), an organization bent on changing the legislative patterns of our nation to secure fair play for women in every area of life.

The Women's Liberation movement is operating predominately on college campuses. This group is articulate about their demands, and some of their literature bears the stamp of the "real honest-to-goodness man-hater." Fringe groups from Women's Lib include SCUM (Society for Cutting Up Men) and the Women's International Terrorist Conspiracy from Hell called WITCH. These new groups seem even more polarized than the old suffragettes. Possibly the fact that we can see them on TV, tossing their bras away and invading government hearings, the vast majority of women find it hard to identify with these activists, even though they might share common concerns.

The presence of such organizations, the ideas they espouse and the actions they propose, are successful in making the American woman evaluate her situation, both publicly and privately. It creates in many women a new awareness of self and gives rise to many questions, the answers to which will affect not only themselves, but their families and friends.

The questions are very basic and have to do with the whole structure of home and family as we have known them. When women are faced with these basic questions, there are varying responses. Some feel threatened and react very negatively to anything that would change the patterns of their lives; others are exhilarated and are anxious to pick up the gauntlet and do battle with the male in his established role of "numero uno."

In a recent issue of *The New Yorker* magazine, there was a droll cartoon by O'Brian.[2] It depicts Eve in the Garden of Eden, looking toward heaven, and a voice from that direction saying, "You are a woman, and I am placing you in complete charge." Looking at it, I wondered if men really think that is what women want, to be in complete charge. I wondered if that was an answer to Freud's famous and oft-quoted question, "What does woman want? Dear God! What does she want?"

In the dim history of societies there was a time when women seemed to be in charge of things. At least the matriarchate or mother family did exist. Descent and kin were recorded through the women, not through men. As Sumner, the grandfather of sociology points out:

> The woman must be thought of as at her home, with her kin, and the husband comes to her. She has great control of the terms on which he is accepted, and she and her kin can drive him away again when they see fit.[3]

The exact time is not known when control of the family and property was taken from the woman.

> It may well be believed that the change from the mother family to the patriarchate or father family is the greatest and most revolutionary (change) in the history of civilization. . . . When the life conditions so changed that it became possible, the father family displaced the mother family. All folkways followed the change. Family arrangements, kin, industry, war, political organizations, property rights, must all conform to the change.[4]

Maybe this was what women wanted, but probably not, because in this arrangement the woman lost the status she had held in the matriarchal society. From these remote times, the woman has been "educated to resignation and endurance."

There followed centuries of societies in which women

were chattel, bought and sold, and accorded little respect in terms of personhood. " 'Blessed be God that He did not make me a woman,' say the Jews in their morning prayers, while their wives pray on a note of resignation: 'Blessed be the Lord, who created me according to His will.' The first among the blessings for which Plato thanked the gods was that he had been created free, not enslaved; the second, a man, not a woman."[5]

John Mills must be especially crowned in heaven, because he was one of the few men in his century or in any century, to take pen in hand and suggest that women deserve to be accorded a more rightful place in this world. His long essay, "The Subjection of Women," was studiously and insightfully written and caused a furor in England. Two years prior to the publication of this book, he had used his influence in Parliament to start the suffragette movement.

On the heels of Mills's breakthrough came the rise of the feminist movement in our own country. Social historians have long been aware that at any time when one disadvantaged group is being given attention and help, at the same time the women begin to move forward again in their struggle for rights and recognition.

Mid-nineteenth century found this young nation in a state of flux. The industrial revolution, the opening of the frontier, and the deep feelings about the existing conditions of slavery were all contributing factors.

Every woman who was to be influential in the rise of the feminist movement got her early training for organizational work in the abolition movement.

Elizabeth Cady Stanton, Lucretia Mott, Lucy Stone, and Susan B. Anthony had all raised their voices in behalf of the slaves. Before the feminist movement was under way, this formidable foursome had learned how to face irate mobs, had been pelted with rotten eggs, hissed and booed, and been given general bad treatment in their concern for civil rights. Some of their efforts had focused on the great temperance movement of the day, and finally it seemed natural that they should work together in a common cause concerning women.

Of all the imposing figures in the fight for women's rights in America, Susan B. Anthony seemed to have the clearest ideas about what she thought women wanted. It was a source of anguish to her and her fellow workers, that women were given no status as citizens of the new democracy. It was especially galling because women had taken great responsibility in the forming of our nation. Without their resourcefulness and backbreaking work there may have been no new nation. The fact that they had done so much and were denied so much fanned the flame that was to burst into a great movement to secure the franchise for women.

Susan Anthony met Elizabeth Cady Stanton following an abolition meeting at Seneca Falls, New York, where in 1848 she (Stanton) and Lucretia Mott organized the Woman's Rights Convention. Their meeting and their instant regard for one another was the first step in a relationship that was to span six decades and bring momentous changes into society. Elizabeth Stanton was a brilliant, logical woman, the mother of three sons. She had her finger in every reform that was going on for civil rights. Susan admired everything about her, especially her facility with words and she became the chief speech writer of the movement.

An incident occurred in Albany, New York, at the state convention of the Sons of Temperance, that gave Susan an impetus to complete commitment on behalf of the women of America.

When Susan and the other women delegates entered the convention of the Sons of Temperance, they looked forward proudly, if a bit timidly, to taking part in the meetings, but when Susan spoke to a motion, the chairman, astonished that a woman would be so immodest as to speak in a public meeting, scathingly announced, "The sisters were not invited here to speak, but to listen and learn."[6]

Susan did not take lightly to this public put-down and the memory of it stayed with her the rest of her life.

Living our comfortable middle-class lives in the eighth decade of the twentieth century, having the right to vote, and the legal guarantee of many other rights, it is hard to imagine the numbers and kinds of battles the valiant women of the nineteenth century fought for us.

According to Alma Lutz in 1854 a father had legal authority to apprentice or will away a child without a mother's consent. The law also required an employer to pay a wife's wages to the husband. It was this kind of injustice that led Susan Anthony to fight for the women in our society to have the vote. She felt strongly that the major way women could come into their own was through franchise. She thought women wanted to vote, but she discovered over and over again that women were her worst enemies.

The ladies of the suffrage movement were caricatured, their personalities distorted in the press. They were ridiculed and made fun of unmercifully, they were accused of being unfeminine in their demands for freedoms; but Elizabeth Stanton and Lucy Stone were both mothers of large families. At one time when Lucy was being pressured to attend a women's rights comvention, she wrote, "I shall not assume responsibility for another convention until I have had my ten daughters."[7]

Susan Anthony's last visit to a national convention was in Washington in 1906 where she celebrated her eighty-sixth birthday.

When asked if she believed all women in the United States would ever be given the vote, she replied, "It will come, but I shall not see it. . . . It is inevitable. We can no more deny the right of self-government to one-half our people than we could keep the Negro forever in bondage. It will not be wrought by the same disrupting forces that freed the slaves, but come it will, and I believe within a generation."[8] She did not live to see the Nineteenth Amendment, enfranchising the women of America, become a reality on August 26, 1920. But she had the satisfaction of knowing it could not have become a reality without the courageous and life-consuming effort she had put forth.

The decade of the twenties was mold-shattering. The heavy "Victorian sheathe" that had encased society began to crack. Girls bobbed their hair, danced the Charleston, and imbibed bathtub gin. All of society took on a new freedom and things were destined never to be the same as before the vote.

The thirties brought the depression years and the attendant concerns that accompany poverty. The job of holding families together left little time for struggles outside the primary areas of concern.

During the forties we found total involvement in the Second World War, but in this crisis women found themselves ably carrying on work that had previously belonged strictly to the males.

After three decades of fluctuation in a woman's life,

the soldiers came home and "Nora ran back to the doll-house." Suburbia flourished and society defined woman's role in terms of home and family once again.

This would have been all well and good if some astute observers of the American scene had not picked up a sense of restlessness and boredom in Utopia. The split-level trap, and Betty Friedan's "problem that has no name" became household words.

I reviewed *The Feminine Mystique* several times before large audiences, and I could visibly see women getting angry. Woman, herself, is the most ardent enemy of the authentic feminist. Most females want their roles defined in a way that makes them comfortable. If the only bastion they have is removed, that is, if their home is not as important as they thought, they feel they have been cheated and left with nothing. If their role as wife-mother is questioned, the very basis of their existence is threatened.

I am intrigued with and concerned with the problems the feminists bring to us, but I must admit I am not an authentic feminist. I believe that most women basically savor the difference between male and female. I agree with Lionel Tiger that there are biological "givens" that influence and shape a deep structure of behavior. I believe, even with the advent of the pill that most women see some truth in Freud's famous statement, "Anatomy is destiny." The presence and use of the pill does not remove the deep instinctual need to reproduce. Biblically there is both support for the "second-sex" theory and the reminder that God looked at his creation and "found it good." Biblically, as well as biologically, we are destined to the role of childbearer. We cannot remove ourselves completely from this primal history. No matter what we decide about ourselves this fact of our being remains.

What do women want? Work, career, vocation may be a part of an answer, but it's not *the* answer. More women are working today, many in extremely challenging jobs, than ever before. But this has not suddenly made their lives integrated into a beautiful whole. Being wife and mother is not the whole answer. This fact is documented daily in doctors' offices and hospitals around the country.

We are human; we're not a race apart, as G. B. Shaw reminds us. We have our human problems. It is this I wish to write about. If the letter of the law has been satisfied, the spirit has not. The spirit of women must be given some attention. In this society, which defines us as seducers and consumers, we must find our way toward growth in all areas of our lives, and toward the fullness of spirit which is our birthright.

It occurs to me that women whose orientation is in the Christian faith might be asking questions now that they have never asked before, concerning their rights and their selfhood. It also occurs to me that their response might be influenced by their spirituality. It is well-known that the organized church has discriminated against women historically. In spite of this, many women find part of their identity to be of a spiritual nature, and the problems they must wrestle with are looked at from that position.

In St. John's version of the new heaven and the new earth, the radiant figure of a woman bearing a child is symbolic of goodness being born again. In our own world of turmoil and hate and war, it is my conviction that women will be the bearers of goodness; that they will be used as instruments in revealing spiritual realities to a weary and tired world. But they cannot be used until they are freed from some of the myths and misconceptions that surround them in our society.

I must write from the Christian frame of reference. Being moved by the Christian experience, what I see I see from that stance. Like Flannery O'Conner, "the engine that runs the machine is faith."

How Society Defines Us

CHAPTER ONE

After Mendelssohn

> With this Ring, I thee wed, with my Body, I thee worship, and with all my worldly Goods, I thee endow: In the name of the Father, and of the Son, and of the Holy Ghost. Amen.
> —*Book of Common Prayer*

Culture is a mirror that defines what our image in society is. It is not a fine plate-glass mirror that sends the reflection back straight and true. It is more like the mirrors in the carnival fun-houses that give us a picture that is out of shape, distorted, yet bearing the stamp of our own authenticity as the source of reflection.

The American bride approaches the altar today weighted down with an image of herself that society has given her. Because of this image that culture imposes, she very likely brings less of a self to her marriage ceremony than she has the right to bring. She has been the victim of a broad cultural discrimination that has shaped her self-image and negated her personhood. Beauvoir, in the introduction of *The Second Sex*, writes,

It is in point of fact, a difficult matter for man to
realize the importance of social discrimination which
seem outwardly insignificant but which produce in woman
moral and intellectual effects so profound that they appear to spring from her original nature.[1]

Our bride is the first product of a total life lived with
the immediacy of communication that the television industry has brought to us. She has been subconsciously and
consciously assaulted by the great advertising complex
since her earliest childhood. She has been taught by thousands of narcissistic images of sex and beauty that her
raison d'être is ultimately to be found satisfying to a man
who will in turn lead her to the altar.

In spite of what else happens in society, marriage re-
tains a sturdy durableness. Just as there are practically no
instances in recorded sociological histories of societies in
which marriage was not a part of culture, it is almost impossible to project into the future the idea of a marriage-
less society, even though extremists in the Women's Lib
movement and the counter culture would have us believe
this.

So the scene repeats itself in a myriad of places, in a
variety of ways. Wherever a wedding is taking place, a sense
of expectancy, a desire of all the participants that this
wedding that is being made on earth really might be made
in heaven, grips the observers. The vows have been spoken,
the prayers sent hopefully in the right direction, the symbols of sight and sound have moved us, all that is left
is Mendelssohn. The mother of the bride wipes a tear from
her eye and mentally prepares for the receiving line. The
father, despite his self-admonition to quit thinking in
terms of dollars and cents, totals things up one more time.
On the altar, the candles are burning with a comfortable

steadiness, highlighting the satins and the shining eyes. The bride, glowing with an unearthliness reserved for this day, and the groom, looking determinedly resourceful under the mantle of new responsibilities, turn for the long walk back. Another American couple has made it to and from the altar. For the bride, a fair question is, "After Mendelssohn, what?"

Behind the American bride of the eighth decade of the twentieth century is a heritage that society has partially hidden from her knowledge. It is the heritage of women of redoubtable courage and undeniable abilities. It is the heritage of the founding mothers and sisters, of the pioneer spirit, of humanitarian goals and world views which can only fill us with admiration.

It is the heritage of a formidable trio, Susan B. Anthony, Elizabeth Stanton, and Lucy Stone, who wrote the Nineteenth Amendment and with dogged persistence handed it to the solons over and over again until finally the American women were given franchise.

But woman has been denied her past and has been denied her heroines, even though they have existed in abundance. She has been denied a sense of history concerning her unique contribution to the developing of her own nation—not only are the heroines of the past almost unavailable to her, but also the contemporary women of great accomplishment are too obscure in a society that places such a high premium on notoriety and sex.

Little boys growing up have a whole battery of heroes with whom to identify. There are the top echelon heroes of statesmen and political leaders, and in the past few years, three national martyrs. There are the heroes of the sports world for boys to measure themselves against and this is a key for many of them to their own developing identity. The collections of baseball cards, the tenacious hold of the Little League spirit that grips whole communities, the household names of Joe Namath and Mickey Mantle, all testify to the importance of heroes in their lives.

And there is another whole category of heroes, the professional man of unusual attainment and merit. This list would include the doctors who made the news with continued breakthroughs in transplants, and the spiritual leaders whose faces are familiar on TV screens. The men who professionally are in action at a high level of performance are known even to the little men of our country.

What boy could not take some heart about himself as he watched the men step on the moon? The very word astronaut conjures in the mind a new frontier and a wonderful kind of raw courage needed to conquer it.

But alas, the little girl, the young lady, the married woman cannot find in our press or TV heroines to match against the heroes. We are limited to the sex goddesses or women who find themselves in the spotlight because of their husbands.

A montage on the cover of a popular magazine depicted the personalities who were instrumental in writing current history. The men represented many areas of activities including politics, religion, sports, science, and industry. Of the women represented only one or two were outside the field of entertainment. The others were the sex goddesses of the movies and television.

It seemed to me that this montage was a true picture of what has happened to the image of women in our culture. It has been in the process of happening for many years, but the idea of the woman as a sexual object only has burst forth in full flower with the help of the "sexual sell" on television. We are left with viewing ourselves in the cultural mirror from a single stance. The illusion of youth, the cultivation of the sexual image to ensure us that the male of the species will be attracted to us constricts our growth to full personhood. We are constantly asked to believe we are important only in our relationship to a man, only in our ability to entice, charm, and maintain ourselves in the constant nymph state.

If this is the truth, then our bride has reached the zenith of her life on her wedding day. She is youthful, in her late teens or early twenties by society's norm; she has managed to attract a male and make a firm arrangement with him in terms of matrimony.

The ads have informed her, and the bridal consultants have assured her, that this is the supreme moment of her life. Granted there is much of the "peak experience" that is part of the wedding day, the ceremony, the honeymoon, but if this is the zenith of her life's experience, then everything else is going to be downhill.

One of the tragedies of American culture is that a woman seemingly moves toward loss instead of gain from this point. Without specific care she will lose the fine taut skin that her youthfulness could boast. By listening to the hucksters (and by following her own deep-down feminine wiles) she can do much to ward off these ravages of loss, but the battle must be a conscious one.

Her interests may be constricted to a circle that loses the depth it once had. She may lose her desire toward growth, and may be self-limiting in the confines of her apartment or house in the suburb. If this occurs, she moves unthinkingly toward loss of a wide range of interests that she once took for granted.

Her children will come, but they will also go, and the loss of these extensions of herself, the vicarious life she may have tried to live through them, is another blow to her ego and self-satisfaction. If the statistics stay true to the mark, she will lose her husband, and that is often the final blow to the self-esteem that was possible through her sexual identity. Figure, face, interests, and husband are all a part of the "born-loser" pattern.

It is a strangely disquieting phenomenon, this focus on youth. In France, a woman is not considered beautiful until she is forty. Seemingly it takes at least that long for the true character, that inner description of life to manifest itself physically so that a woman can be known to be beautiful from the inside out.

This seems a saner approach for the female to live with, a saner concept to bring to the altar. It gives her leeway for growth and helps her to move toward gain instead of loss, as she is always in the process of becoming something better, more mature, wiser, and more beautiful than she has been.

That society does force us into patterns of thought and action is clearly recognizable as we look outside ourselves and into other cultural situations.

Russia is an interesting example of what another culture has done to the image of women. When the Communists came to power over fifty years ago, women were given equal status with men, including equal opportunities for education and the pursuing of goals.

With the horrendous man-power loss that Russia suffered in the Second World War, the Russian woman, by necessity, was further elevated in the professional life of the nation.

At the present time, 75 per cent of the doctors in Russia are women, 66 per cent of the teachers, 40 per cent of the scientific workers, and 30 per cent of the engineers. While this involvement in a career presents the Russian woman with a whole new set of problems, it also means that she is forced to move into new experiences and all that it takes to keep abreast in the working world.

The following conversation was recorded in an article in the magazine *Soviet Life* and indicates the kind of image that men in Russia have formed of women, because of society's changed attitudes toward them.

Somebody wanted to introduce me to a girl, twenty-two, a beauty with an angelic character. "What does your angel do?" I asked. "Is she in college or working?" "Neither," I was told. "She couldn't get into college, tried and failed three times. And she doesn't have to work because her father is the director of a bank." "What does she want?" I asked. "To get married," I was told. "That's not enough of a goal, is it?"[2]

Whether or not marriage, an institution to which I am fully committed, is enough of a goal or not, is not the point here. The point is that a woman need not be considered from the limited stance of her sexuality. She deserves the same opportunity for the nurture of her aims and goals as a man has. Whatever we may dislike about the Communists, they have allowed their women the luxury of heroines. They have, at the same time, also made their women work in factories and coal mines and have given them a monopoly on the business of sweeping streets.

On my eleventh birthday, my mother gave me a small book entitled *Girls' Stories of Great Women*. It was not a great book in the literary sense, but it opened a whole new world to me of women who had persevered and overcome great odds in life to be what they were intended to be.

Of a whole assortment of personalities including Jenny Lind, Clara Barton, Helen Keller, Susan Anthony, and many others, I identified with Jane Addams. For years I was spellbound by her life, and many decisions I made, including my course of study in college, were related to the influence the knowledge of her contribution made on me.

Our society should give us our heroines, should give us images and ideals against which we can relate our own identity. Any number of women are leading lives of heroic proportions today in terms of their life styles and the contributions they make to society. As long as we are limited by the focus on the sex-goddess image, our own identity suffers.

Life is characterized by change, growth, and movement. If a woman yields to the pressures of culture and to the demands of society, she negates her own life and diminishes her concept of self.

CHAPTER TWO

Fluffy, Just Fluffy

Not huffy, or stuffy, nor tiny or tall,
But fluffy, just fluffy, with no brains at all.
—A. P. HERBERT

The great advertising complex of America seems to have
gotten its directive concerning women from the opinions
of A. P. Herbert. The women of America are victims of
one of the greatest put-downs in the history of our society.
If we were to believe what we see in the ads, our image
would be one of brainless, witless, narcissistic dumbbells.
What even makes this reality more frightening is that
thousands of dollars are spent by the mass producers trying to figure out what will get to us. And in the process of
psyching us out collectively, they come up with answers
that most women, who are at all aware of what is going on
on the TV screens and other media of communications,
must find insulting and frustrating.

The evolution of the female via the ads is an interesting
phenomenon to observe. The little girls are adorable and
clever, all bright and sparkling—the kind to which any
parent would like to lay claim. The teen-agers are wistful

and lovely, always dreaming of that day when they will be a "woman." They seem intelligent and exhibit an unusual sense of awareness. The young adults (late teens, early twenties) are really sophisticated, beautiful, and demure. But at any age level above that the woman suddenly turns into some strident-voiced creature whose biggest problem is what kind of soap to use on her clothes. She whines and covets her neighbors' whiteness and brightness, and is finally relieved of her wash-day agonies by the right detergent.

One cheerful idiot, all decked out in ostrich feathers, rolls on her newly waxed floor, chortling sensually about this magnificent product. The neurotic preoccupation she pretends with a clean floor must be nauseating to an intelligent viewer. Granted the ads use extreme methods to get a point across, we still have the right to feel insulted when we are exploited in such a tasteless manner.

Every facet of our lives is examined by the ads. Our physiology is examined from our need for the right deodorant and toothpaste to our need for a specific laxative. Our social life is examined by our ability to keep house as well as the gal next door. And we may make it on the social scene if we shape up and use the right brand of coffee. In the process of the examinations we all seem to suffer from arrested development, from a narrow constricting frame of reference.

I am familiar enough with the free enterprise system to understand the contribution advertising makes to the process. What makes me respond negatively is a consistent, determined effort to underrate the intelligence of women. Whether or not the effort is conscious eludes me, but one can only conclude it must be, since it pays such striking dividends.

Men are not characterized in roles in the ads that make

them less than men, that treat them as bodies only or as individuals obsessed with the smallness of life. While women are photographed in advertising for the sole purpose of a public viewing of bodies, men are always photographed engaged in some activity, sports or business. Even if it is only elbow bending at the bar, men are doing something, while women offer a body to be exploited and used. The spirit of a man, his identity in work and meaningful activity is given cognizance. Women should expect as much from a system that is dependent upon them as consumers to keep the great wheels of finance greased and moving.

One gets a strong impression from the ads that women are only concerned with themselves or things, that they are never engaged in any worthwhile pursuits or endeavors except those defined by the sexual role. When one considers that 42 per cent of American women over sixteen are now working in jobs outside the home, the credibility gap between the ads and the reality of our lives is rather awesome. If we were to accept the Silva-Thin cigarette advertisement we would be led to the conclusion that the best women are "thin and rich." Bulova's Accutron ad shows a plain but perfectly acceptable-looking girl typing at the rate of sixty or seventy words a minute. The man, holding a stop watch and obviously checking her qualifications, says rather disdainfully, "We'll let you know." At another typewriter a leggy, blond-model type is using the hunt and peck method. Guess who got the job in the world of the "sexual sell"?

Jules Henry, in a tremendously insightful book *Culture Against Man*, has this to say about the exploitation of women in our system:

"Are we wasting women?" queries *Life* editorially. The answer is, of course, No! No nation on earth has ever used them to greater advantage. Without the pecuniary uses of women, their hair, their faces, their legs and all the wondrous variety of their personality and anatomy, the economy would perish. Even the armaments race would not save it, nor could we eat enough nostrums to make up for the loss of the monetized female. But along with monetization, along with their power to hurl the economy to unimagined heights, woman has been degraded. How can she permit advertising to portray her as it does? Why does she not rise up in rage? Perhaps her idealization of herself prevents the American woman from perceiving what is actually happening to her.

Of course, I do not argue that such degradation was alone responsible for the tremendous and unexpected rise in gross national product. What I do urge, however, is that women, by permitting themselves to be degraded, by allowing their most intimate privacies to be exploited, have made a formidable self-sacrificing contribution to national well-being. The recesses of the feminine soul have become ransom for the gross national product.[1]

The ads proclaim, "You've come a long way, baby, to get where you've got today." The dubious goal is a certain brand of cigarette, and the message is clear. We've come a long way to know such freedom of choice. Perhaps we have not come such a long way. In the American system of advertising, we are collective chattel, sold daily on the block of the nation's money-making pursuits. It is this in part that produces the rage that spurs on the serious feminist. She refuses to be chattel in the twentieth century, and hopes she can help her sister to see the light.

Women's magazines form another part of the cultural mirror in which we find our image reflected. The slicks include the big three, *Ladies' Home Journal, Good House-*

keeping, and *McCall's,* which have a combined circulation of over twenty million readers and presumably cater to the philosophy of total womanhood. *Redbook* and *Cosmopolitan* get their share of the female eye, but they are presented in a little different format. There are others, of course, concerned with homemaking and fashion.

An interesting cultural history of women could be written through the documentation of changes in these magazines in the last fifty years. Betty Friedan pointed out some of these changes in *The Feminine Mystique.* While some of the basic values remain the same, there has been an obvious shift in the type of article which gets most attention. An even more noticeable change occurs in fiction, one change being that there is less fiction being published than in past decades. Another change is in the role of the heroine; her character, aspirations, and dreams have shifted with the demands of culture. In describing the change in heroines, Friedan writes,

> These new happy housewife heroines seem strangely younger than the spirited career girls of the thirties and forties. They seem to get younger all the time, in looks and a childlike kind of dependence. They have no vision of the future, except to have a baby. The housewife heroines are forever young, because their own image ends in childbirth. Like Peter Pan, they must remain young, while their children grow up with the world.[2]

Armed with two or three good women's magazines, a bride can still learn to cook, get clever ideas for decorating a home, and indulge her creative moods in a variety of arts and crafts. Via the written word she could visit with a gynecologist, a psychiatrist, and a baby doctor, preparing herself for the probable role of motherhood. Information on how to keep a husband, almost as difficult as getting one in the first place, is available. With careful reading she can find insight into her role as satellite to her husband and, reaching beyond the confines of their relationship, she can get pointers on making good impressions everywhere. Related to this are great hordes of information about the body, how to stay young, beautiful, and thin forever and ever, Amen. It is an exterior view of herself that she is faced with, and this makes life dull!

TV's impact on our society is so immediate and so penetrating that it has changed almost every agency of our culture. The result has been that even the women's magazines have had to fight back. The stolid guardians of hearth and home and morals for generations have succumbed to the demand for the sensational. Where once the intimate lives of the movie stars were explored only in that special breed of magazine, the movie pulp, now the women's magazines almost always feature an article concerning a personality or personalities from movie or TV land.

In an interesting issue of *McCall's*, January 1970, the editors featured the theme, "The Good Life on Earth." Some of our finest writers wrote minuscule editorials on this subject. But much of the issue was given over to the good life of the famous and notorious. One of the articles, entitled "The Good, Good Life of the Alpine Set" concerned some ten or eleven film stars and the esoteric lives they lead in Switzerland where the tax structure is of benefit to them. In the same issue a page each is devoted to Barbra Streisand, Steve McQueen, Harry Belafonte, Lee Marvin, Bill Cosby, Mia Farrow, and Joanne and Paul Newman, and the quest for solitude to which success and fame has driven them.

The women's magazines, which at one time contributed

to a woman's development of a world view through articles that were "idea" based, now cater almost entirely to looking at a woman from the vantage point of her sex. This involves attention to her body and getting and keeping a man. It also provides her with sensational news of the jet set and movie stars, because if her life is so limited by this imposed image, then there must be some surcease from boredom by reading about people in a never-never land of glittering society, fabulous jewels, and uncountable riches.

A sampling of lead articles from one of the top three women's magazines shows their preoccupation with the above subjects. On the cover of the January and February 1970 issue of the *Ladies' Home Journal* we find the following titles: "The World's Easiest Diet" plus "Advice from the Formerly Fat Psychiatrist," "Why I Named My Son after Robert Kennedy" by TV star Andy Williams, "Women Who Look Younger Than They Are," "The New York Life of Jackie Kennedy Onassis," and "My Good and Bad Times" by Glen Campbell. On the October 1969 frontispiece we find "The Bosom, A Modern Woman's Guide," "The Girl in Ted Kennedy's Car," and "Unfaithful Couples Tell How Adultery Starts."

While there is much talk about freedom and the new woman, the mold in which we are inevitably cast seems more permanently set than ever.

Helen Gurley Brown is quoted in the magazine *Town and Country* (September 1969) as saying,

> We're missing the boat by not taking advantage of all the things that are finally ours. Why aren't more women doctors and bank presidents? Why aren't more women "real" heroines? The heroines today aren't the Amelia Earharts or the Eleanor Roosevelts—they're the women

who don't do anything but give parties or go to them.
Lady Bird Johnson had to play down the fact that she
made millions because this wasn't a good image. I think
we shouldn't feel guilty about exercising our capabilities.
It's fun to be a leader, to have people need you.[3]

I recorded this quote, because as editor of *Cosmopolitan*
Helen G. Brown views women almost entirely from the
sexual stance. In a single issue of her magazine, January
1970, we find the following subjects explored: "Yes, You
Can Have Bigger Bosoms," an article about silicon breast
augmentation; "Everything to Do in Your 20's to Stay
Young and Beautiful into Your 40's and 50's"; the "Mia
Farrow File"; "What Will Be Sexy in the 70's," and a
dubious article entitled, "How to Be a Bitch and Make
Men Like It."

This article, written by W. H. Manville, is introduced
with the following blurb:

All girls play the role some of the time. Some unfor-
tunate girls find themselves cast into it most of the time.
But no really hip woman wants to be a bitch all of
the time. It just doesn't pay. For special situations, however, (and we all have those), an occasional bitchy act
is necessary, and works . . . if you do it with style, intelligence, and female grace.[4]

Having been taught that style, intelligence, and female
grace elevated one above such a goal, this idea seemed
absurd by normal standards.

In another article entitled "Watch Your Dates," sug-
gestions such as the following are made:

For daring girls who are willing to extend themselves,
invite a man to dinner in honor of save the pun week.

(January 4–10) Act out a pun. Appear topless, saying
this is your way of keeping abreast. He may become
your bosom buddy before dessert.[5]

And another proposal in the same whimsical vein raises
the youth cult a notch higher and demeans age considerably:

Heaven forbid! You've lost your man to an older woman?
Invite them both for lunch. Explain you made the gesture in honor of "Old Lady Day." Watch her squirm![6]

Do all of these things make any real difference in our
lives? I think they do. That we are being manipulated by
forces outside ourselves in our system is common knowledge. Our psyches have been delved into; we have been
studied at depth levels to find out how we will respond to
advertising techniques, and to what Vance Packard so aptly
calls the "Hidden Persuaders." Unconsciously we are victims of ourselves, by our own response to the very things
that negate us. As a woman yearns toward growth and
fulfillment it would seem that she needs to be very dis-
cerning about cultural values around her. She needs to be
aware that what she reads and looks at as a steady diet
often minimizes her as a person. In a real sense, to clarify
our identity and to grow in personhood, we need to fight
back at culture, to decide what we will be lest the demands
of the ads, the TV, the women's magazines decide for us.

CHAPTER THREE

If Women Had Written Stories

By God! if women had written stories
As clerks have with-in his oratories
They would have written of men more wickedness
Than all the mark of Adam may redress.
—CHAUCER, *The Wife of Bath*

The Wife of Bath had great insight into the literary situation of the thirteenth century regarding women. How fascinating that her words ring so true in the twentieth century. Men still write most of the books, and they still use their stories to write wickedness of women.

Our literary heritage from the Greeks and Romans, and from the Judaic-Christian point of view is the fountainhead of the misogyny that has always existed in the written word.

In the creation story from the Greeks we find Zeus creating Pandora because Prometheus had angered him. Because he cared so much for his own kind, Prometheus gave the best parts of the sacrifice to men instead of to Zeus.

In a grandiose retaliation,

> He made a great evil for men, a sweet and lovely thing
> to look upon in the likeness of a shy maiden, and all
> the gods gave her gifts, silvery raiment and a broidered
> veil, a wonder to behold, and bright garlands of bloom-
> ing flowers and a crown of gold—great beauty shone out
> from it. Because of what they gave her they called her
> Pandora, which means the "gift of all." When this beauti-
> ful disaster had been made, Zeus brought her out and
> wonder took hold of gods and men when they beheld
> her. From her, the first woman, comes the race of women
> who are an evil to men, with a nature to do evil.[1]

Whether Pandora's wickedness or curiosity led her to opening the box that contained the plagues and sorrows of
mankind is not firmly established. What is of prime importance in the myth is that the onus is on Pandora for
inflicting evil on men, who, until her fated appearance,
were gamboling through the Golden Age.

The comparison between this story and the biblical con-
ception of the creation is well marked. Adam dwells in
Paradise until God creates for him a helpmeet, "for it is
not good for man to dwell alone." When the serpent convinced Eve it was all right to go ahead and eat of the fruit
of the tree of knowledge, was it wickedness or curiosity
that prompted her to do so? The outcome bears striking
similarity to the Greeks' concept of creation. It is Eve's
fatal error that causes Adam to be expelled from Paradise,
that brings them both face to face with painful self-knowl-
edge, and that leads God to decree that Adam must earn
his bread by the sweat of his brow. Eve bears an even
greater punishment. God speaks to her in that perfect
habitation which she must now leave, saying,

I will greatly multiply your pain in child-bearing; in pain you shall bring forth children, yet your desire shall be for your husband, and he shall rule over you.

The wisest men do not know where the myth ends and truth begins. But we do know that these stories that create the backdrop of civilization point out that woman is not just a helpmeet or companion. Somewhere deep in her being there is supposedly some special "alien darkness" that makes her a natural enemy to man.

In the literature of the ages, the hostility and aggressiveness that men would feel toward a mortal enemy manifests itself in diverse ways. From the Bible, the brilliant and eloquent classics down through the spectrum of the written word, to the cheapest little jokes about marriage and mothers-in-law, the invective men feel toward women is obvious. The road from Adam and Eve to "Momism" is paved with wicked women out to do men in. Sons, lovers, husbands—none is spared by the "beautiful disaster."

Histories have been written on this subject, and many a Ph.D. candidate has delved deeply into the whys and wherefores of misogyny in literature. It is neither my desire nor purpose to vie with scholars of literature or psychology on this point.

I have a real interest, however, concerning the contemporary scene because, like advertising and journalism, the literature we pursue helps create the cultural climate in which we live.

In the past decade, writers including Tennessee Williams, Gore Vidal, Vladimir Nabakov, Norman Mailer, J. D. Salinger, Philip Roth, and Edward Albee, to name only a few, have given us some grotesque and degrading characterizations of womanhood. There is an art to cursing women, and these men have wielded their extraordinary talent with brilliance. I was interested in the reaction of a reviewer who found himself faced with a novel that was the opposite of the usual mysoginistic fare which we support. He reviewed a first novel by Gail Godwin, and while admitting it to be an "excellent piece of work" he says, almost with a whimper,

> The women in this novel are, all of them, more or less interesting, more or less sympathetic. The men, starting with the doctor (who is, as John Fowles has observed, "an only too convincing male monster"), are all fatuous and self-centered creatures. This is then, a woman's novel in a narrow and constricting way.[2]

If this be true, then libraries are filled with "men's novels, in narrow and constricting ways."

To pursue my idea further, I would like to discuss two or three literary events of the past decade that have made some impact on society.

Who's Afraid of Virginia Woolf? began a long run on Broadway in October 1962, and was destined to prove a real triumph for its author, Edward Albee. He received practically every award given for drama that year except the coveted Pulitzer prize.

The title of this play, a biting parody of "Who's Afraid of the Big Bad Wolf?" is more important and more organically close to the contents of the work than most titles are. Virginia Woolf, a brilliant author and critic of late nineteenth- and early twentieth-century England, was the kind of woman of whom most men are mortally afraid. She could and often did match her intellect against the great men of her day, and she was the guiding center of the cerebral and artistic Bloomsbury group. It was Virginia Woolf who was once refused entrance to Bodleian Library at Oxford. The library itself was a great symbol of the quest for truth, and to refuse women this quest seemed to her an outrage. Her anger at this happening was the springboard for her feminist lectures, unmatched yet in wit and acumen, "A Room of One's Own."

So the answer to the question raised at the faculty party, "Who's afraid of Virginia Woolf?" was, "Practically everybody." The men whom she might emasculate with her razor-sharp mind, and even the ladies, the professors' wives who could not compete with her wit and independent spirit.

This drama is basically a love story in the marital setting, but the love is layered in hostility, disillusionment, and hate. Martha, a daughter of a successful and powerful college president is encased in bitterness. That her husband, George, has remained an ignominious professor instead of rising to the heights that "Daddy" has is one of the chief sources of her anger. But a deeper scar is caused by her inability to have children. She has assuaged this wound by creating an illusion of a son, which George has allowed and abetted; this has become the most serious game they play.

The entire action of the play takes place in George and Martha's living room following a faculty party where the song, "Who's Afraid of Virginia Woolf?" was sung and received a hilarious response from the guests.

Martha invites a young faculty couple, Nick and Honey, to drop in, and the action builds up in a series of brutal games, including "Get the Host," "Get the Guest," and "Bringing Up Baby." The brutality manifests itself as each character is stripped of more and more pretense until they are psychologically naked in front of the others. The final revelation occurs when George announces the death of their illusory son, thereby depriving Martha of the most visceral illusion of all. It would be difficult to imagine a more shrewish, sadistic wife than Martha. She makes use of language with the deadly intensity that she would a fine weapon. In line after line, she carves away at George, denigrating his intelligence, his sense of humor, his social aplomb, and his professional life. At one point when Martha is bragging about her capacity as compared to his for liquor, George admits that he has given to Martha all the abomination prizes there are to give. She retorts by bringing George's very existence into question, calling him a blank, a cipher, and a zero.

Martha's language and action are both so brutal that we have to delve deeply to find a point from which to sympathize. While George is the main target, neither Nick nor Honey can escape the violent verbal slashing that occurs. As if her own characterization did not vilify her sufficiently, George leaves no doubt in our mind that we are face to face with a not so "beautiful disaster." He openly admits he is worried about her mind and threatens to commit her. In one scene where they declare total war, which will end with George's victory, he refers to her as a monster, spoiled, self-indulgent, willful, dirty-minded, and liquor-ridden.

In one of the most pathetic soliloquies in recent writing, Martha gets to the heart of the matter, her own self-hatred that governs her seemingly irrational actions. Using Martha's feelings about herself, the author indicates the polarities that exist between a good man and a bad woman.

While Martha reviles herself as one who gives all the wrong responses to George when he reaches out to her, she speaks of him as being good to her, loving, and compassionate. In a final burst of self-revelation, she suggests that the unforgivable thing that George has done has been to love her, and for that basic error he must be punished.

As the play finally ends, and finally is not misused here, because hostility in such full measure is not pleasant to watch, all the illusions and delusions are gone. One is informed in various ways that underneath the hostility there is love present, and that something good may still be nurtured between them. In the last moving scene as George touches Martha and sings very softly to her, "Who's afraid of Virginia Woolf?" she answers, "I am." Martha was an educated woman, shrewd and intelligent. She has right to fear that of which she has become capable, and that is closely related to her intellect. There are mysteries yet unfathomed in this domestic tragedy. Obviously, Martha is not the kind of a girl a boy would want to take home to Mama. Her creation as a character is ignoble and degrading, and it says more about the men who write about women, than the women of whom they write.

In 1963 Charles Webb wrote a slight little novel called *The Graduate*, which passed by largely unnoticed by the reading public. Several years later it was made into a movie that attracted phenomenal crowds around the entire nation and created a new household word, Mrs. Robinson. While it seemed particularly relevant to the college-age group, old and young alike flocked to see Benjamin and Mrs. Robinson glumly carrying on their affair at the Hotel Taft.

The story is a simple one with few wry complications, hilarious to read or watch if you do not think too much about what is happening.

Benjamin Braddock comes home to California after graduation from a famous east coast college where he has amassed considerable victories, both scholastic and athletic, to a lawn party which his parents are giving in his honor. He is a most reluctant guest; the values of the upper-middle class as echoed in the surroundings and the other guests get to him; he feels his parents treat him as if he and his honors were status symbols, adding to their own prestige with their homogeneous friends. Benjamin escapes the stifling atmosphere in the confines of his own room, where he wants to "just think about things."

Among the guests are Mr. and Mrs. Robinson. Mr. Robinson is Benjamin's father's partner in business and has been for a number of years. Mrs. Robinson seeks Benjamin out and does not exactly lure him into taking her home. She rather insists on it, offering herself to him for an affair. Benjamin, out of decency and respect for his parents, escapes her first offer, but after a few weeks of boredom and aimlessness he sets up a meeting with Mrs. Robinson at the Hotel Taft. These meetings continue throughout the summer and are brought to a screeching halt when Benjamin falls in love with Mrs. Robinson's daughter, Elaine.

These complications and the solution to the problems posed by such an unlikely *ménage à trois* is the denouement of the book. Benjamin literally drags Elaine away from a wedding which her mother and father have engineered, and in the last scene, Elaine, her bridal veil awry, and Benjamin are riding away on a local bus that happened along at the right time. This is a book/movie about the hypocrisies of our value system, the alienation and aimlessness of the young intellectuals, and Mrs. Robinson.

Mrs. Robinson, in spite of the fact that she is the central female character in the book, is a sort of nebulous creature. Her identity is difficult to grasp—she seems to have no deep center that defines her for herself or the reader. She is not sufficiently wifely to be identified through her husband or sufficiently motherly to be identified through Elaine. This is all to the good, provided she is

sufficient unto herself, but such is not the case. She comes
to us as a shadowy character, lacking substance or purpose. We know she is an alcoholic, and that her marriage to Mr. Robinson was made out of necessity. Her
disenchantment with him is of long standing. We know,
too, that she is a bored and unhappy woman, and that
Benjamin is a victim to her needs.

Her liaison with Benjamin is one motivated singularly
from her desire for sex. There is an almost completely
non-verbal relationship, never progressing beyond the
amenities wherein Benjamin addresses her as Mrs. Robinson. In desperation, after several weeks of silent meetings,
Benjamin suggests they might indulge in conversation,
but Mrs. Robinson feels they have nothing to say to
each other. One is gripped by the predatoriness of Mrs.
Robinson's character, seeking and victimizing the boy, un-
able to share in any human concern of his own needs.
She seems to be amoral rather than immoral, with a
detached disregard for any effect her actions might have
on others. The only time she shows any deep feelings
is when she vehemently forbids Benjamin to ever see
Elaine.

In an impersonal culture, Mrs. Robinson comes off as
a woman incapable of relating to persons beyond the most
superficial level. The loneliness, detachment, and apathy
we sense in our mechanized society are all a part of Mrs.
Robinson.

Benjamin's mother, another middle-aged, attractive female, seems strangely divorced from the reality of her
son's world. Her lack of insight into his problems is an
all too-familiar look at the upper-middle-class mother, obsessed with things, and concerned chiefly with the impression she and her family are creating on others.

Elaine, the young college girl, is a different story. Like

the separation we get on TV between youth and age, the middle-agers in this story are fey and fickle, but the daughter is almost perfection personified. She is tender and sweet, sensitive about her parents, submissive, and not too smart. (A fact of which she keeps reminding Benjamin.) It is almost impossible to see an organic connection between Mrs. Robinson and Elaine, even though they are mother and daughter.

Along with Martha and Mrs. Robinson, the 1960s have given us a whole new catalogue of fiendish females, including Portnoy's Mama and his girl friend with the descriptive name, The Monkey. Myra Breckenridge was the most unlikely heroine to come down the literary pike. Ada spent her life romancing her half-brother, and Rosemary gave birth to a devil. There were countless others of stripes inane, immoral, and outlandish.

A little known feminist of the seventeenth century, De la Barre is quoted in *The Second Sex* as saying,

> All that has been written about women by men should be suspect, for the men are at once judge and party to the lawsuit.

We must bear in mind that by stereotyping women in inferior ways, men have the satisfaction of cheering on their own egos. Men still write about wickedness of women and part of the anger of the Women's Lib movement is directed at this phenomenon in our culture.

While our individual characters may be neither deceived nor thwarted by what we read, we need to always be aware that our victimization in the written word keeps happening with startling regularity.

CHAPTER FOUR

Second-hand Adam

Woman is the female of the human species, and not
a different kind of animal.
—GEORGE BERNARD SHAW

The definition with which culture clothes us is one of
obvious limitations and strictures. By this definition we
are indeed Second-hand Adams, the object instead of the
subject. Viewing ourselves contemporarily, society says we
are "essential only in our inessentiality"; as adjuncts to
man, either to do his will as a slave does the will of a
master, or to be worshiped atop a "great phallic totem."
Both polarities are repugnant to most women, and would
not by their very nature be attractive to the spiritually
oriented woman.

The confusion women feel about their identity today
is not something that arrived overnight like the succulent
mushroom. It has been a long time coming—the result
of myth, of societal conditioning, of trying to break the
mold of sexuality, only to be forced back into an even
more rigid mold.

George Bernard Shaw gets to the heart of the problem in his aphorism, "Woman is the female of the human species, and not a different kind of animal." It is this sense that has been with us through countless centuries that we are a race apart that brings our humanness into question. We have been conditioned to believe that man is human and we are something else, though we are not quite sure what.

Simone de Beauvoir, writing in *The Second Sex*, says:

Thus humanity is male and man defines woman not in herself but as relative to him; she is not regarded as an autonomous being. Michelet writes, "Woman, the relative being . . ." and Benda is most positive in his "Rapport d' Uriel," the body of man makes sense in itself quite apart from that of woman, whereas the latter seems wanting in significance by itself. . . . Man can think of himself without woman. She cannot think of herself without man. And she is simply what man decrees; thus she is called "the sex," by which is meant that she appears essentially to the male as a sexual being. For him, she is sex, absolute sex, no less. She is defined and differentiated with reference to man and not he with reference to her; she is the incidental, the inessential as opposed to the essential. He is the subject, he is the absolute, she is the other.[1]

If we feel that somehow things have changed considerably and women no longer should feel like "second-class citizens," we need only remind ourselves that not a great deal has happened to change concretely our situation since 1848. At that time Lucretia Mott and Elizabeth Cady Stanton were holding forth at the first Women's Rights Convention at Seneca Falls, New York. A Declaration of Sentiments drafted by Mrs. Stanton began with the hopeful suggestion,

> We hold these truths to be self-evident, that all men and women are created equal.

Of the reforms called for in the Declaration, which included the right to vote, to equal education and vocational opportunities, suffrage is the only desire to have been met some 122 years later.

A reporter writing in *Time* magazine, of August 31, 1970, offers the following statistical information to underline the "relentless second-class" position that the women who comprise 51 per cent of the American population still hold:

> A third of the American work force is female; forty-two per cent of the women sixteen and older work. Yet there is only one economic indicator in which women consistently lead men, and that is the number living in poverty. In 1968, the median salary for full-time year-round workers was $7,870 for white males, $5,314 for non-white males, $4,580 for white women, and $3,487 for non-white women. The median wage for full-time workers is 58.2 per cent of that for men. Translated into educational levels, women make half of what men do; on the average, a woman needs a college degree to earn more than a man does with an eighth grade education.

Along with this secondary place in the working world, another category comes to mind. It is of interest to consider the world of the arts, where creativity and originality are the premium. While there have been a number of good women novelists, poets, and artists, there appear to be very few women geniuses in recorded history. There are fewer female geniuses than male, but there are also fewer female idiots than male, which is heartening.

The facts are available to us but the explanations for the differences still elude science. Presumably, societal conditioning has kept many a potential female genius from full development. Stendahl is quoted as saying, "All geniuses who are born women, are lost to the public good." On the other hand, the expression "genius will out" bears testimony to the fact that given whatever elusive combination of brilliance and madness and creativity genius comprises, it will reveal itself because it can do no other.

In the case of the child prodigy, practically every prodigy the world has ever heard of is male. There are three areas of attainment that most often produce the prodigy: music, mathematics, and chess. There seems to be a relationship between these three pursuits. Each of the three involves patterns—the arrangement of notes in music, the arrangement of integers in math, and the arrangement of pieces on the chess board. Why a genius level of performance in these disciplines should manifest itself in little boys rather than in little girls is an intriguing question. Is there something about being female that disallows prodigious development in these areas? Maybe little girls are not programed for patterns. How early cultural conditioning takes over in the sexes has never been clearly shown, but it would have to be very early to block the development of prodigious talents.

Subconsciously and very early the little girl learns that she is living in a man's world. Virginia Woolf suggests that "the most transient visitor to this planet who reads an evening paper could not fail to be aware that England was under the rule of a patriarchy." She writes,

Nobody in their senses could fail to detect the dominance of the professor. His was the power and the money and the influence. He was the proprietor of the paper and its editor and sub-editor. He was the Foreign Secretary and the Judge. He was the cricketeer; he owned the racehorses and the yachts. He was the director of the company that pays two hundred per cent to its shareholders. He left millions to charities and colleges that were ruled by himself. He will decide if the hair of the meataxe is human; he it is who will acquit or convict the murderer, and hang him or let him go free. With the exception of the fog, he seemed to control everything.[2]

Simone de Beauvoir reminds us that for greatness to flower, one had to feel at home in this world, to come to terms with the world, examine it and deal with it. The limitations put on woman in her position as the "other" keeps her from this kind of development. She lives in the shadows of the accomplishments of one who has "transcended her transcendence."

She goes on to say,

We can count on the fingers of one hand the women who have traversed the given in search of its secret dimension. Emily Brontë has questioned death, Virginia Woolf life, and Katherine Mansfield—not very often—everyday contingence and suffering. No woman wrote *The Trial, Moby Dick, Ulysses,* or *The Seven Pillars of Wisdom.* Women do not contest the human situation because they have hardly begun to assume it. This explains why their works for the most part lack metaphysical resonances and also anger; they do not take the world incidentally, they do not ask questions, they do not expose its contradictions; they take it as it is too seriously. It should be said that the majority of men have the same limitations; it is when we compare the woman of achievement with the few rare male artists who deserve to be called "great men" that she seems mediocre.[3]

An interesting fact that is recorded in *The Second Sex* is that out of a thousand statues in the city of Paris (excepting the Queens) there are only ten raised to women. Of these ten, three are consecrated to Joan of Arc. I was speaking one time on the subject of creativity to a group of college women, and I used that bit of information to make a point. A dear lady at the back of the room, mother of seven doctor sons, interrupted me. "But you must remember," she said, "that women gave birth to those nine hundred ninety men." I thanked her for her insight and continued speaking.

And I truly think it was insightful. It is possible that women have never been challenged by the creativity in arts as have men, because they are "creators" in the primal sense. It is possible that they are more at home in this world than men are, because they help create the world. It is no accident that Nature is referred to as the absolute feminine, "Mother Nature." Perhaps the great spiritual enterprises in which women are naturally involved are sufficient to her.

In the act of childbirth and in the subsequent acts of nurture, much creativity is naturally expressed. This may satisfy the human impulse for creativity. Most women may feel no need to go beyond this ultimate act of creation for gratification. I am sure one of the reasons that natural childbirth is so popular is that women get the full awareness of the mystery and greatness of creativity.

I remember a reaction I enjoyed following the birth of both of my daughters. I was engulfed with the sense that this was a "first," that in some unique solitary way I had experienced what no one else had ever experienced. Knowing this to be absurd from a rational point of view, I checked with friends who had recently had children, and discovered that they, too, had indulged themselves in the same emotion. This was evidence of the highly creative forces at work in our lives, for surely the artist, the writer, the composer, the poet understands this sense of solitariness in the creative venture.

Virginia Woolf suggests that women are not allowed to be creative in the arts because their accomplishments would diminish those of men. She says:

> Women have served all these centuries as looking-glasses possessing the magic and delicious power of reflecting the figure of man at twice its natural size. Without that power probably the earth would still be swamp and jungle. The glories of all our wars would be unknown. We should still be scratching the outlines of deer on the remains of mutton bones and bartering flints for sheepskins or whatever simple ornament took our unsophisticated taste. Supermen and Fingers of Destiny would never have existed. The Czar and the Kaiser would never have worn their crowns or lost them. Whatever may be their use in civilised societies, mirrors are essential to all violent and heroic action. That is why Napoleon and Mussolini both insist so emphatically upon the inferiority of women, for if they were not inferior they would cease to enlarge. That serves to explain in part the necessity that women so often are to men. And it serves to explain how restless they are under her criticism; how impossible it is for her to say to them this book is bad, this picture is feeble, or whatever it may be, without giving far more pain and rousing far more anger than a man would do who gave the same criticism. For if she begins to tell the truth, the figure in the looking-glass shrinks; his fitness for life is diminished.[4]

While one may conclude from the facts of society that women collectively are second-hand Adams, that is only part of the truth. Another part of the truth has to do with individual women living out their individual lives who have not succumbed to the myths or the exterior forces that would compel them to be less than they are intended to be.

In the introduction to *The Second Sex*, Beauvoir says,

> If woman seems to be the inessential which never becomes the essential, it is because she herself fails to bring about the change.[5]

We are living in an exciting period of history when woman is trying valiantly to effect this change. As I write this, the Women's Equal Rights amendment approved by the House is being further delayed in the Senate while the opponents search fruitlessly for an alternative. The clarity of the amendment, "that equality of rights under the law shall not be denied or abridged by the United States or by any state on account of sex" makes one wonder what alternative the men are seeking. While we are collectively involved in these broad changes that will eventually raise the status of women, significant changes are being brought about in our lives at very personal levels.

The woman's role in civilization has been remarkably static. She has been the child-bearer, the housekeeper; the nurture of hearth and home has been her domain as far back as the light of history can expose us to ourselves. Man's role has changed much more dramatically as he moved from a hunter to a farmer to an industrial animal. The tools he handled, the work he did, the basic quality of his life changed more noticeably than woman.

Now woman is experiencing more dramatic changes in her role than in any previous period of history. The mechanical aids with which she is surrounded change the

nature of the work load with which she is faced. The
access to the public media supplies her with a world
view that was never possible before. The amount and
quality of education available to her has reached new
heights. The fact that she has almost complete control
over the size of a family allows her freedom in struc-
turing her own life in ways that have not previously been
available to her. More than ever before she can be self-
determined. She can make choices in the light of new
knowledge and new conditions that are beneficial to her.

Most of the women I know are not just fluff—they
are not basically neurotic or selfish. They rightly resist
being categorized and they resist stereotypes. Many of
them have a deep understanding of their reason for being.
They may be second-class citizens collectively, but in-
dividually they are living first-class lives. If we are inessential, it is because we are willing to be. If we are
slaves, it is because we are willing to be. Women's liberation is an interior thing, and it is our own responsibility to liberate ourselves to freedom and its attendant
growth.

How We Define Ourselves

CHAPTER FIVE

A Flower or a Stone

Let them think I love them more than
  I do,
Let them think I care, though I go
  alone,
If it lifts their pride, what is it to me,
Who am self-complete as a flower
  or a stone?
  —SARA TEASDALE, *The Solitary*

There is a strange lingering sense of bitterness in the words of Sara Teasdale but they say a great deal about identity. One hears so much about the identity crisis, but one hears very little about what identity is.

In the previous chapter, I have tried to show the different ways in which society, through ads and magazines and books defines the American woman. The identity she gets from these outside forces is not very flattering to her development as a whole person. But her identity is not dependent on these extraneous sources. Much of what she is as a person comes to her in her various attitudes toward

life and the people to whom she is in the closest relationship.

There is a sense of completeness about one who has
a true sense of identity, a strong sure center of being
that holds fast regardless of outside forces. In an obscure
piece of literature a woman in her later years describes
herself in this manner, "The house is getting old and
badly needs repair, but the same little girl is looking out
the windows." That's identity.

Virginia Woolf readying herself for the barrage of crit-
icism she would face on the publication of a new book
said,

> The *Westminster Gazette* will be hostile; so, very likely,
> the *Nation*. But I am perfectly serious in saying that noth-
> ing budges me from my determination to go on or alters
> my pleasure; so whatever happens, though the surface
> may be agitated, the center is secure.[1]

That's identity.

One of my friends became a legend in her own life-
time at Manchester College. Sadie Wampler had such an
array of talents and such strength of personality that she
left her mark on hundreds of students as well as on the
institution. She was an artist, a musician, and a dramatist,
and each facet of her talent was used to spur relentlessly
toward excellence the students who came her way. Shortly
after she reached middle age, her exterior manner of living
was altered by crippling arthritis. Students would troop
to her home instead of a classroom, and there in the
intimacy of her personal surroundings, she continued to
teach. When I met Sadie she was approaching her seven-
ties, twisted and bent and bedridden. Occasionally, with
the help of a couple of men, she would be put into a
wheel chair and taken to some special occasion. On her

seventy-fifth birthday I had a party for her. While wheeling her in her chair the short block between our two homes, I said, "Well, Sadie, how does it feel to be seventy-five?" She answered very quickly, "I don't feel any different than I did when I was twenty-five." That's identity.

William James in his *Principles of Psychology* says,

> In its widest possible sense, a man's Self is the sum total of all that he can call his, not only his body and his psychic powers, but his clothes and his house, his wife and children, his ancestors and friends, his reputation and works, his land and horses, and yacht and bank account. All of these things give him the same emotion. If they wax and prosper, he feels triumphant; if they dwindle and die away, he feels cast down,—not necessarily in the same degree for each thing, but in much the same way for all.[2]

Anything that is an extension of ourselves is tied to us with strings of emotion. That is why we feel so much pain when our children are feeling pain; that is why we can be critical of our husbands, but we would fight anyone else who assumes that privilege. Even our material possessions take on an aura of self, and we feel demeaned if someone comments negatively about our house or our clothes, or anything that is the extension of the precious "I—Me—Mine." It occurs to me that the surer one is at the center of his being concerning his selfhood, so the various extensions of self diminish in proportion to the strength of the central core. But the difficulty of separating self from all these related persons and things remains, thus identity is an inclusive term.

Perhaps the single most important way we achieve identity is in our relationship to others. Erik H. Erikson, the psychoanalyst, reminds us that identity begins "some-

or a woman?

where in the first true 'meeting' of mother and baby as two persons who can touch and recognize each other, and it does not 'end' until a man's power of mutual affirmation wanes."

James refers to the recognition one gets from his mates as a person's "social self" and he suggests that "no more fiendish punishment could be devised, were such a thing physically possible, than that one should be turned loose in society and remain absolutely unnoticed by all the members thereof. If no one turned around when we spoke, or minded what we did, but if every person we meet 'cut us dead,' and acted as if we were non-existing things, a kind of rage and impotent despair would ere long well up in us, from which the cruelest bodily tortures would be a relief; for these would make us feel that, however bad might be our plight, we had not sunk to such a depth as to be unworthy of attention at all."[3]

There is something very beautiful and satisfying about a complete woman. The completeness, to be sure, is tied up with her own sensations of self, and what confirmation she has had from other people concerning herself. That is why the woman, particularly in the wife-mother role, plays such an important part in the lives of others. This importance cannot be minimized because she is in the spot where she literally gives identity to other people.

She constantly (and often unconsciously) is in the process of confirming the selfhood of others. The expression on her face, the gesture of affection, the words of approval she gives to her children are a way of continually helping them to build their own egos, to feel that they do exist as persons, and that others are aware of them. The expression on her face may negate a person, her gestures might be gestures of contempt rather than of affection, and she might use a vocabulary of disapproval rather than approval. If a woman fails to confirm the selfhood of the people closest to her, this can literally result in a "loss of self" to the extent that the person becomes ill. In this sense, women have a responsibility that has a great bearing on the social health of the nation.

The breakdown in personality as we see it today, the delinquents and societal misfits are often individuals who have not been confirmed by an important adult in their lives. We must never be guilty of minimizing the long-range significance of a woman's availability and approving presence in the task of making children grow into their "humanness."

In a study of human communications this observation of R. D. Laing is quoted:

> The characteristic family pattern that has emerged from the study of families of schizophrenics does not so much involve a child who is subject to outright neglect or even obvious trauma but a child whose authenticity has been subjected to subtle but persistent mutilation, often quite unwittingly.[4]

It follows that the surer a woman is of her "self," the more of a self she will have to give to the people around her. It seems important for women to know how responsible they are for their children's sense of identity. A daughter gets her whole idea of sexuality, femininity, and "womanness" from living with her mother. She absorbs attitudes and characteristics at a very early age that will stay with her forever, and will be the major influence in her life as mother and wife. She will use many of the same techniques in raising her own children; her

attitude toward discipline will be almost identical to what
she has known; she will carry on the same traditions if
she has been lucky enough to be the recipient of such.
I am sure most women have been in the midst of some
response to their children and they have been struck by
the fact that they were "re-enacting" their mother's life.
I have often thought "shades of Julia" as in my reprimands
to my daughters I heard myself sounding exactly like my
own mother in days when she was unwittingly confirming
my identity.

By the same token, a son will get identity as he sees
his mother in relation to the father. From his father
he will get his pattern of sexuality and manhood, but
the mother plays a large role in the boy's developing
identity. As she juxtaposes her femininity against his developing masculine sense, he begins to understand himself in relation to women.

There is great confusion in our society concerning the
masculine-feminine role. There is a rising rate of homo-
sexuality which is closely related to the "dominant
mother" or the kind of woman who has taken the male
role in the family. The psychoanalyst, Erik Erikson, dis-
cussing in *Childhood and Society* the origins of this matriarchal development, feels that "Mom is more the victim than the victor," and that the American mother was
forced into a position of power because the father, at
work in the city five days a week and around the house
only on weekends, abdicated the central position in the
family. "Mother became Mom only when Father became
Pop."[5] He is talking here about the generation of mothers
whose children are now between twenty and fifty and
not about the present generation of mothers whom he refers to as being "confused."

*husband the
means*

Some of the confusion might be/dispelled if woman
gave her primary attention to the male in the household.
Since a child's growing identity is partly found in what
he observes in the male-female relation of his parents,
the way a woman responds to her husband carries over-
tones of the responsibility she bears to her children.

One can sit in almost any hair-dressing salon in the
country, listen to the conversation that is going on, and
make some general deductions about American women.
Of course, these are generalizations because not all women
go to the beauty shop and not all beauty shop conversation
is pure untarnished truth; still one can glean a grain of
truth hovering in the cloud of hair spray.

The number one item of discussion is children. A great
deal of attention is focused on their accomplishments,
their witticisms, and the busyness of their little lives.
Following this in order of importance, women talk about
their houses, the spring cleaning and gardening, the decorating, a new item of furniture or new "things" in general.
Sometimes clothes get in the conversation, occasionally
books or a particularly apropos magazine article, but seldom are husbands discussed. When they are it is usually
in an off-hand manner, reporting some ridiculous thing
they did or said. One definitely gets the idea in a beauty
shop that husbands are not the hub of women's lives, the
center around which they build varying kinds of security
for themselves and their children.

It is no secret that ours is a child-centered society, but
there are inherent dangers in this kind of emphasis. In
a child-centered society both parents tend to think that
the axis of the universe goes right through their little
darlings' heads, and subsequently all life revolves around
junior. The perils and pitfalls of such fuzzy thinking are

obvious, and the child is no genuine benefactor in such an arrangement. If the wife focuses on the primary relationship between herself and her husband, she establishes a better atmosphere in which her children can experience growth as persons.

One of the sureties that was in the possession of my sisters and brother and me as we were growing up was the surety that my father was of chief importance in my mother's life. This did not seem in any way to diminish the way she felt about us or the love she freely gave; it was that he was of first interest and concern to her. My mother was not an Aunt Tabby in any sense. There was about her a remarkable completeness; she was no second-hand Adam. She had a career as a registered nurse and worked at various intervals during my growing-up days.

In subtle ways we were informed that Roy and Julia were one and then there were four more of us. I recall as a very young child that her day moved toward the time when "he" would arrive home. The ritual of my sister Kate and me waking from our afternoon naps and getting scrubbed and polished for "his" arrival was significant to us. The house was put in order because "Daddy likes the house to look nice," the meals were cooked with accompanying comments, "this is your dad's favorite," in continual ways and gestures we were informed of how important he was to her.

One has only to read various advice columns in our newpapers to get the message that the husband in many American homes is the "displaced person." In one column written for retired people there are constant questions concerning husbands who are "in the way," who upset the routine "I've established," who make themselves too comfortable around the house thereby destroying the "motel lobby" image the wife has struggled for in her living room. I find this all very sad, that a relationship that began with promises to love, honor, and cherish through all the vicissitudes and joys of life, has degenerated to this level of living.

In other situations there is very present the feeling that the husband is thought of primarily as the one who brings in the things, and that the only excuse for him to be part of the family rests on his fulfilling their materialistic longings. While he may be the provider, there is something rather demeaning about his being solely that, that negates him as a person and moves him away from the central position in the family.

When I talk about a wife focusing on her husband as the chief person in her life, I am not talking about a woman being a slave to a man, or a woman kowtowing to every whim that might strike her husband.

I am talking about a woman with enough sureness about herself to be able to give to her mate the kind of support he needs to rightfully take his male role in the family structure. It is the unspoken message that says to children, "I chose this man because I love him. It is to him that I owe my first allegiance. Because I love him and committed myself to him I choose to make him the central person in my life." This kind of message also says to the children that they will be moving themselves toward a commitment to another person. Because of societal changes, the commitment may not be made in the same marital context that exists today. But it would be difficult to imagine any kind of society in which individuals did not make choices of persons that would involve some kind of firm and lasting relationship.

To make the kind of total commitment that is called for in marriage, a woman has to operate from a strong sense of self. If she can do this, her husband, her children, all of the people to whom she relates will be better people for her being what she is.

CHAPTER SIX

The Placemaker

"Home is the place where, when you
    have to go there
    They have to take you in."
    —ROBERT FROST, *The Death of the Hired Man*

I have a recurring dream in which I am returned to a place of my childhood. It is an ordinary house on an ordinary street, one of several in which I grew up. In the dream it appears in remarkable clarity. I walk down the street, up the walk and through a side door which takes me directly into the dining room. Through a cased door, the living room is visible, the furniture arranged with the strange exactness of buried memory. In the dining room, a sewing machine occupies a prominent place, and hanging in the doorway between the dining room and kitchen are two new dresses that my mother has completed on the open machine. I stand there in quiet satisfaction because of the dresses and wait for people—my mother and father, sisters and brother to appear. They never do. It occurs to me that this dream says something about the importance of places in our lives. What

deep subconscious tale is being told here eludes me, but
that this particular place was of more import than I
consciously grasp seems clear.

In the midst of societal upheaval such as we are now
experiencing, we are confronted daily with the sense of
rootlessness, alienation, and "un-belonging" that occurs
when people do not have a sense of place. While love is
the chief emotional need we have, a sense of place may
be second unto it, because much of our psychological
strength, our identity, is found through place. Paul Tournier in an insightful book entitled *A Place for You* says,
"To speak of deprivation of love is to describe a purely
psychological event. The human person is more than a
psychological mechanism, his life is more than his emotional psychic life. Deprivation of place makes us feel the
materiality, the incarnateness of all the events of our
lives."[1]

Tournier points out how easy it is for us to feel displaced; to walk into a restaurant and not find a place
to sit; for a child to enter a schoolroom and have to
wait for the teacher to find him a place while the eyes
of all the other children are upon him; to enter a meeting only to discover that the chairs have all been taken
and momentarily, at least, one is without a place. If
we recognize trauma even in this limited kind of dis-
placement, then we have some idea of the horrendous
trauma suffered by the "displaced peoples" following
World War II, when they were uprooted from home, from
country, from all that was familiar and thrown on to the
mercy of the world to find a place for them. Early in
the Old Testament, where place-names have such great
significance and strengthen the reality of what we read
there, God punishes Cain for the murder of Abel, saying,

"You shall be a fugitive and wanderer on the earth"
(Genesis 4:12).

We see in this act the importance ascribed to "place"
and the subsequent suffering in being deprived of a place.
In *The Man Without a Country*, the tragedy of Philip
Nolan's life is that he must wander forever on the high
seas, going from one vessel to another in his lonely exile,
as his punishment for traitorous deeds. To be mentally
as well as physically deprived of even a country to call
one's own is almost more than mortal man can bear.

I have a dear friend who seems utterly secure within
himself, secure enough to face with equanimity whatever
might be doled out to him on his pilgrimage. His family
farms the same plot of ground in Italy that his ancestors
were farming six hundred years ago, and it seems very
obvious to me that much of his strength, which I find
so admirable, comes from having an undeniable affirmation
of "place" in his life.

The place need not reach high standards of architecture
or decorating to be of import. It becomes significant as
the location where one's personhood is confirmed. A man
responded to a photographer who had gone to the ghetto
to record poignant human experience on film by saying,
"What you call the ghetto, I call home." Any place where
relationship exists and identity is given reality becomes
significant to people.

If we grasp the importance of "place" in the building of identity and the nurturing of personhood, then we
understand the significance of the woman as a "placemaker." Tournier says, "Man is an incarnate being who
needs a place and who needs to be firmly attached to
it."[2] He goes on to point out that without women, men
live in monasteries, barracks, or slums. This idea is rem-

don't you notice sexism, Helman?

iniscent of the Chinese proverb, "A hundred men may make an encampment but it takes a woman to make a home." As we move in our own country from a predominantly rural to a predominantly urban society, we lose the quality of life that a sense of being "rooted in a place" gives us. Mobility is a key word often used to help define our society. People are constantly on the move, on to different jobs and locations so that the emotional value of having one's roots down, in a specific and permanent residence, is denied to many.

In the rural society one is more likely to find clans; family members will have a larger group of people on whom they can lean for support—their "place" is both enlarged and enriched by the presence of large numbers of people who care about what happens to them. But as people have become more mobile and more urbanized, the security and support of the presence of grandmas and grandpas and aunts and uncles and cousins is almost removed from them.

When I was growing up, if a crisis arose in the family, such as serious illness, there were numerous relatives ready to help by their presence or by removing us children from the scene. We always had playmates available to us in the form of cousins, and though we moved from house to house in a specific area, we had a strong sense of place, of being rooted in this particular vicinity and being supported socially and morally by large numbers of people.

In just one generation, most of the cousins who grew up together have moved away from this sure center of place to urban situations where a vocation called them.

In a recent report from the Center for the Study of Democratic Institutions, Eulah Laucks, following a study of the American family, suggests that the changes this sacred institution is undergoing at present are so profound as to threaten its very existence.

> The idea of family extensions in purely "blood-tie terms" has exhausted itself. . . . A very real possibility is the transitional family, an ongoing development of many experimental forms stemming in general from the basic parent-children core and expanding to include various combinations of non-related people of mixed ages who just happen at a given time to live in the same vicinity. . . . Random in its make-up, such a family would be homogeneous in ideals and purpose.[3]

Our own personal experience gives credence to these changes. My daughters have grown up isolated from any family except their parents. They have had to be what Jules Henry calls their own "social engineers," because a ready-made social structure has not been available to them —the playmate-cousin situation has escaped them entirely. On important occasions such as recitals, graduations, etc., we find substitute aunts and uncles in families who have been friends, but this is not as deeply satisfying as the old family structure was.

With this mobility and rootlessness in mind, one sees how important it is that someone establish a sense of place. And this someone is woman, the mother, the wife, whose very presence indicates a "place" is possible. One time when we had moved from a large imposing house into a small apartment, my mother was sitting forlornly in the middle of the packing boxes, the tears flowing down her cheeks. My father came in and seeing her he said, "Why, Julia, what's the matter?" "Oh," she cried, "this little place just doesn't seem like home." Dad went over and put his arms around her and said, "Julia, any place where you and I are together is home."

Erik H. Erikson did some fascinating experiments some years ago by his usual method of observing play-behavior, this time in pre-adolescent youngsters. His chief interest was the observation of spacial configurations in relation to stages of the life cycle. Using a number of toys, a family, uniformed figures, automobiles, wild and domestic animals, blocks, furniture, etc., the children (150 boys and 150 girls observed three times in a two-year span) were instructed by Erikson to construct a scene. The children were asked to imagine that the table was a moving-picture studio; the toys, actors, and props; and they themselves, moving-picture directors. They were to arrange on the table "an exciting scene from an imaginary moving picture."[4] Erikson noted that "girls and boys used space differently, and that certain configurations occurred strikingly often in the construction of one sex and rarely in those of the other. The differences themselves were so simple that at first they seemed a matter of course. History in the meantime has offered a slogan for it: the girls emphasized inner space and the boys outer space."[5]

In this emphasis of inner space, which of course bears a somatic resemblance to the womb, the girls constructed their scenes in the following manner:

This then is typical: the girl's scene is an interior scene, represented either as a configuration of furniture without any surrounding walls, or by a *simple enclosure* built with blocks. In the girl's scene, people and animals are mostly *within* such an interior or enclosure, and they are primarily people or animals in a *static* (sitting, standing) position. Girls' enclosures consist of *low walls*, i.e., only one block high, except for an occasional elaborate *doorway*. These interiors of houses with or without walls were, for the most part, expressly *peaceful*. Often a little girl was playing the piano. In a number of cases the *interior was intruded* by animals or dangerous men. Yet the idea of an intruding creature did not necessarily lead to the defensive erection of walls or the closing of doors. Rather the majority of these intrusions have an element of humor and of pleasurable excitement.[6]

oh shit

These experiments indicate that there may be an inherent need in women to be a "placemaker," to set the scene where the procreative and nurturing process may go on.

Answering his critics before they spoke, Erikson says,

It should be clear, then, that I am using my definitions concerning the central importance of woman's procreative task not in a renewed attempt to "doom" every woman to perpetual motherhood and to deny her the equivalence of individuality and the equality of citizenship. But since a woman is never not-a-woman, she can see her long-range goals only in those modes of activities which include and integrate her natural dispositions. . . . True equality can only mean the right to be uniquely creative.[7]

I cannot think of another time in history when the placemaker is more significant to the people around her. In this world where everything that was nailed down has come loose, where confusion is the undisputed king, where value systems are suspect at every level, the security of a sense of place, a little home to "jo to," as the old mountaineer said, cannot be overestimated.

Being the placemaker is a significant ministry that seems to belong uniquely to the woman. If the place were significant only in its physicality, its content, or its sanitary condition, then it would not matter much who kept the house. But there are ramifications of a place far beyond what we can see. That is why it is so difficult to pass judgment on family life. Some home situations that seem impossibly dirty or low standard or seem to lack the presence of a woman at crucial times still manage to be good homes. Some home situations that seem perfect from the outside looking in, orderly, clean, a mother who manages to stay home all the time, do not always prove to inspire the greatest family life. Oftentimes where open conflict and hostility is in evidence, things still seem to work out, while in homes that are havens of quietness and peace, things go badly. The quality that marks the difference between success and failure in family life is extremely evanescent.

In our little town some families take children from the ghetto during the summer weeks to get them into the freedom and sunlight of middle America. An adoptive mother remarked to a group that she hated to think of the child she had kept going back to the situation from which he came. She thought there might be an element of cruelty in our showing them the good life, only to send them back to ghetto living. One astute listener asked if the child had a mother. When informed that he had, the listener remarked, "Don't worry too much about it. He would rather be in the ghetto with Mama than with strangers in suburbia."

If a woman understands the deep psychological needs of her family in terms of a "place," then part of her fear that she will be just a "housekeeper" can be waylaid. One can be just a housekeeper if one chooses, but if a woman is a wife and mother, she must be able to see beyond the "thingness" of a place into the spirit of the lives of which she is a center.

The home has always been the symbol of that "place" where people are gathered in, where one gets some surcease from outside pressures, where bruises are healed and crooked places are made straight. There is a balm in Gilead. In Robert Frost's poem "The Death of the Hired Man," a husband and wife are having a conversation about the hired man who has come back to their farm to die. The wife says, "Home is the place where, when you go there They have to take you in." And the husband responds,

"I should have called it
    Something you somehow haven't to deserve."[8]

The new awareness of women concerning their lives as manifested in the Women's Liberation movement, has made them extremely sensitive about their roles as the placemaker or homemaker or whatever name you wish to call it. In their search for identity many women have not found the home satisfying and are searching beyond this for their fulfillment. Many other women, because of the economic situation of America, find themselves working outside the home as a necessity. One discovers in a working situation, however, that the woman is still the hub of the "place," and her attitudes and feelings set the stage for what happens at home.

When Paul Tournier's mother died he was only six years old. As a result of her death, which left him and his sister orphaned, they were taken to live with an aunt. During the trip, he said to his maid who was taking them, "Shall we never be going back to Place Neuve?" His question was a question of place, but it was much more than that. It was a question concerning his whole life pattern—not should we never return to Place Neuve, but shall we never see her again? Shall we never play here again? Is our home as we have known it to be completely removed from us? This incident is reported in Tournier's book A *Place for You*.

It reminds us that there are few people in this world who do not long for a place—who do not need a place. If a woman provides that place where complete acceptance abides, where the advocate is ever-present, where healing occurs, where reality is faced, where joy is paramount, she finds a key to her developing identity. Not only is her own identity made more secure, as she succeeds as a "placemaker" other lives are touched and strengthened, and in a very real way she is contributing heavily to a better society.

CHAPTER SEVEN

The Eye and Mind for Beauty

To see the world in a grain of sand,
And a heaven in a wildflower;
—WILLIAM BLAKE

We were caught high in the Smoky Mountains in a storm of such severity that we were forced off the road by high winds and a driving rain that completely obscured visibility. We sat and waited the storm out and after what seemed a very long time we were able to start down the mountain. Suddenly the sun burst through the grayness and wetness, and the girls were shouting, "Oh, look at that rainbow!" My husband pronounced it the most brilliant rainbow he had ever seen and Bunny and Dawn, with great exclamations of delight, agreed with him. I was nonchalant. It was a nice rainbow, but it seemed to be not that much different than other rainbows I had been privileged to see. My family was disappointed in me—they kept urging me to speak in superlatives that matched theirs concerning this beautiful phenomenon, but in honesty I could not. At the bottom of the mountain we found a small restaurant that was satisfactory, and went in, little tensions about the rainbow encircling us. When the waitress handed me a menu and I started to read it, I suddenly realized I was wearing dark glasses. Then it became clear why I had not seen the rainbow in all its brilliance as had the rest of the family.

It occurred to me that many people exist in a perpetual state of wearing dark glasses, and fail to perceive with clarity the beauty that is a continual part of life. This lack of awareness dulls the mind and spirit and contributes to a pattern of boredom that seems a waste of life's precious energies.

A story is told about Leo Tolstoy walking with three of his schoolboys on a moonlit night. There was snow on the ground, clouds were scudding across the sky, and the teacher and his pupils were skirting the edge of the woods where the wolves roamed. Tolstoy related an experience he had shared with the brave Cossacks. He told of one of the soldiers who was completely surrounded by his enemies. Knowing death was certain the Cossack broke into song and threw himself on his dagger. Tolstoy's young friends were struck by the idea of a man singing in the face of death. One of them presented these questions to his master: "Why does one learn singing? What is drawing for? Why write well?" The teacher couldn't answer at that moment, but he thought about these questions for the rest of his life. Some thirty-seven years later he tried to explain the mysterious relationship between art and life in a lengthy essay entitled "What Is Art?" He reached the same conclusion that Plato had earlier expressed, and he said that which every creative and aware person innately feels, namely that "art is not an ornamental addition to life, not a pleasure, or solace, or even an amusement. Art is an organ of life—a vital func-

tioning part of life which enables man to transmit his
perceptions into feeling. It has the unique function of
uniting humans in love of each other and of life itself."

To be aware of the many facets of art in our daily
experience is a means of the enrichment of life. Awareness and its attendant benefits is another key to identity,
because the person who is truly aware, physically and
psychologically, is led naturally to a greater knowledge of
self. The spirit of awareness with which women live makes
a difference in the various roles they are destined to play.
As the placemaker, the wife, mother, or friend, one brings
to bear upon a home and relationships the resulting benefits of awareness.

Some years ago at the University of California at
Berkeley a comprehensive study was made concerning
creativity in human beings, and was subsequently reported
in the *Saturday Review* of February 10, 1962 by Donald W.
McKinnon. Over a period of six years psychologists studied
three hundred highly creative persons engaged in pursuits
from the areas of both the arts and sciences. One of the
things that this research indicated was the fact that
creative people operate at a very high level of awareness.
That is, their perceptions of sight and sound were keen
and they kept them well-honed by continuous use. Dame
Edith Sitwell describes a poet as one who has managed
to retain the sharp sensory perceptions that he had in
childhood. Children do see things with enviable clarity,
the blue sky is truly blue, the green grass a vibrant green,
the fall leaves are gathered and explored with an intensity that adults seem to lack. It is obvious to most people
that a child is marvelously aware of the world around
him. A child speaks in metaphors, dawdles because he's

making observations, doesn't watch where he is going because he is aware of some point of interest that his adult counterpart will pass by.

I presume a fair explanation for this discrepancy lies in the fact that the older one gets, the more one is distracted by the need to study or work, or just by the routineness of life that often engulfs and represses us.

In January 1959 *House Beautiful* did an entire issue on the subject of awareness. One of the interesting exercises in awareness they showed through the use of photographs of the most prosaic subjects. These included pictures of a glass in dishwater, the light being caught in a prism of the crystal to create a beautiful rainbow within the glass. There were photographs of the lowly onion and a close-up of the cross section of a green pepper, which was reminiscent of a great cathedral window. The object of this, of course, was to sharpen our senses, and to remind us that beauty of line and form is at our fingertips daily. A challenge I used to give my junior-high pupils was to suggest that they try to find a straight line in nature. Since the curve is more aesthetically pleasing than the straight line, how pleasant for us that our eye usually beholds the curved line. It is an awareness of line, form, and texture that adds meaning to our days and makes a difference to us as placemakers. "He who celebrates not the world of things is starving his own soul of a large access of the meaning of life."

One of the differences of our lives as compared with the lives of our grandmothers and great-grandmothers is that their existence forced them into awareness. It was of necessity that they were creative, and in their creativity, awareness was a natural by-product. The clothes their families wore were products of their own hands, the food their families ate was cooked without benefit of prepackaging. All the things that made survival on the frontier possible were things that challenged a woman's creativity and sharpened her sense of awareness of the world around her.

I have a coverlet that was woven by my husband's great-grandmother and has become a treasured family heirloom. This coverlet which was woven from purely practical needs involved every process for this woman from the raising of the sheep to the tying off the last bit of warp and weft from the loom. It was necessary for her to card and spin the wool, a highly creative process, that according to a modern-day spinner I know, is intensely exciting and satisfying. She made the dyes that were used to color the wool she had spun, and I imagine that her search in the woods for the nuts and berries she would use was aesthetically pleasing to her and strengthened her awareness of beauty. Her decision of a pattern and the subsequent task of threading the loom were creative tasks that sharpened her awareness of line, that led her into thoughts concerning texture, all of which were surely soul satisfying. And when the lovely coverlet was finished and removed from the loom, her accomplishment was obvious and of great psychic benefit. It is doubtful she knew her work had been so well done that it would last for generations, but she could not have failed to have been pleased with the fruit of such a variety of labors.

I write all this to acknowledge that in the technocratic society in which we find ourselves, this kind of deeply satisfying venture is almost totally removed from us. In the world of the ready-made and ready-to-use and instant everything, those very things that filled a woman's days with a sense of her worthiness and her necessary presence to others are in a large sense gone. Instant cake manufacturers have discovered it is better to leave one step, the adding of a fresh egg, for the consumer to do. Cake mixes to which one need only add water do not sell as well as cake mixes to which one adds an egg as well. Evidently there is in this prosaic act something that makes the woman feel she has helped to create the finished product, and that feeling is important to her. We no longer need to be creative to survive physically, but psychologically this deep need remains and we are better women if we heed it and do something about it. Awareness of our surroundings, of line and form, of beauty and texture is something we can encourage in our children. The more perceptive we can help them to become, the more they will develop a self-awareness that is a part of their growing identity. Children are not always terribly responsive to another's perceptions, but it would be wrong not to share the important experiences of life with them. At Point Betsie in northern Michigan where we vacation yearly, the sunsets over Lake Michigan are of such beauty that they defy description. Each evening the family gathers on the beach or a dune to watch this glorious phenomenon. One evening when Dawn had been invited to do something with a friend, I heard her decline, saying, "We have to go to the beach. My mom's got a thing about sunsets." The kind of awareness I'm speaking of is not limited to things, but includes people, ourselves, and others. It is not limited to the sharpness of one's physical senses but includes one's perceptions into personality and into human relationships.

If our physical senses are sharpened, that is if we are truly perceptive about our physical surroundings, then it seems to follow that our psychic awareness is also stimulated. In the study of creative persons that I mentioned earlier this was proven to be true. Creative people seemed to possess an openness to experience, not only their own experiences but those of others. They seemed genuinely interested in other people, and their own self-awareness seemed to make them less threatened by others or defensive.

As our perceptions are sharpened this cannot help making a difference in the way we view ourselves. The creative person in the study was "given to expression rather than to repression or suppression." This lack of repressive influence in one's self opens up all sorts of access to experience, both conscious and unconscious. McKinnon points out that the person who has clear self-perception is aware of psychic disturbances in life. This does not indicate an imbalance of personality, because everyone lives with some psychic disturbance. Rather it suggests the willingness to give expression to psychic disturbance, and it is often "revelatory of the richness and complexity of personality." The persons who are creative are usually willing to reveal a great deal about themselves; they are open and free and do not fear self-revelation. "They demonstrate clearly what clinical psychologists have long contended: that personal soundness is not an absence of problems but a way of reacting to them."

According to the report, Jung gets the psychological processes in life down to two, judging and perceiving. If one reaches a high level of awareness, one tends to perceive instead of judge. This art of perception rather than judgment gives one access into the personalities of others as well as one's self. A non-judgmental person needs fewer defenses, and people learn they can relate to a person with this quality without jeopardizing their own personalities. This fact of awareness alone has great fringe benefits for the placemaker. For a woman's life is basically a life of relationship—whether it is relating to her husband or children, or a variety of friends and relatives and colleagues, she finds herself in constant relationship. If she can approach people with an openness that perceiving rather than judging gives to her, then she will be a person who strengthens others. When a woman understands and gives cognizance to the physical world, loves it and is aware of it, and when she understands herself, then she is open and ready for satisfying relations with others. The most interesting women I know, the most alive women I know, are truly aware—aware of the beauty of life and the beauty of personality.

When *House Beautiful* magazine devoted an issue to awareness in January 1959, the editor Elizabeth Gordon wrote an opening letter in which she said in part:

As I watch people struggling to endow their daily lives with significance and beauty, it seems increasingly clear to me that the key to successful living is awareness. It is the insensitive ones who make the mistakes in taste, who serve the tasteless food, who blunder socially. It is the insensitive who are bored and fatigued by their boredom. It is almost as though they were dead, because they are living only a fraction of the life that is potentially within them.

The ones who are alive, who find everything interesting, are the ones who have developed a high degree of awareness. Their homes are always filled with beauty, no matter how low their incomes. They never have empty time on their hands because they are pursuing so many fascinating projects. They find life exciting, no matter their age or social status or educational record. They have learned how to see and to seek. They have achieved the most lasting of riches: They have made the thrill of discovery, which can occur again and again because there is more to discover than can be encompassed in ten lifetimes.[1]

Many women find creative satisfaction in managing a home. The possibilities for the creative acts of cooking, sewing, decorating, and other domestic facets of expression are sufficient for a host of women.

Others need a different way of expressing their creativity, and many look to the challenge of a job that makes use of specific training or talents. Myriads of jobs available to women are a channel for a variety of interests, and a woman should have the freedom to decide how she can best satisfy her basic need for creative expression.

In a small prayer book entitled *Bless This Mess and Other Prayers*, the authors, Jo Carr and Imogene Sorley, in reference to the "paint by number" pictures available now, suggest that one can't paint by number all of one's life. What the life of awareness really calls for is a whole new abandonment to the creative way of life, with the individual choosing to do those things which will be a unique expression of herself, thereby strengthening her own identity.

CHAPTER EIGHT

The Heart for Truth

My mirth can laugh and talk
but cannot sing:
My grief finds harmonies
in everything.
—JAMES THOMSON, *Two Sonnets*

The community in which I live is an idyllic-appearing place with wide tree-shaded streets and homes that are well maintained. There are the combined luxuries here of space and clean air, as well as the questionable advantage of a homogeneous society. The problems of the big cities, of overcrowding and pollution and traffic jams seem very far away. But in one way this little community is not unlike the metropolitan area. In the depersonalization of the metropolis, people wear masks, and they wear masks here too. They are often masks of satisfaction about their homes and children and husbands and wives and their way of life. So successful are the masks that are assumed that when we first moved here, I thought I had been cast into a veritable midwestern paradise.

In the more constricted college community of which I was a part, it seemed that all the marriages were units of perfection and the children scrupulously well behaved. There seemed to be no place for that which would jar the façade of this little Utopia. Of course, reality will have its way, and I soon found that behind the masks were the same tensions and fears and disappointments that plague all of us. For women to grow in freedom and to foster a strong sense of identity, they must be less dependent upon masks and more willing to search for the truth about themselves.

Sigmund Freud said, "To be completely honest with oneself is the very best effort a human being can make." There seems to be a willingness, even a need for humans to be honest with themselves. Parents of adopted children are urged to level with them concerning their situation because people have a deep need for integrity and truth concerning their own condition. In Rollo May's book *Man's Search for Himself* he reports the ancient classic concerning Oedipus' search for self-truth in the following manner:

Schopenhauer well refers to King Oedipus as his illustration of the tremendous courage necessary to see truth, and the statements of Jocasta, the wife and mother, as the temptations to avoid seeing truth. Oedipus, determined to clear up the terrible mystery that he suspects surrounds his birth, calls in the old shepherd who had many years before been ordered to kill him as a newborn baby. The shepherd is the one man who can solve the question as to whether Oedipus has really married his mother. In the words in Sophocles' drama, Jocasta tries to dissuade Oedipus:

   . . . Best take life easily,
   As a man may . . .
   Why ask who 'twas he spoke of?
   Nay never mind—never remember it.
When Oedipus persists she cries,
   Don't seek it! I am sick and that's enough! . . .
   Wretch, what thou art O might'st thou never know!
But Oedipus is not to be put off by her hysteria:
   I will not hearken—not to know the whole . . . .
   Break out what will, I shall not hesitate,
   Low though it be, to trace the source of me.
When the shepherd cries,
   O, I am at the horror, now, to speak!
Oedipus rejoins:
   And I to hear. But I must hear—no less. When Oedipus
learns the horrible truth that he has killed his father and
married Jocasta, his mother, he puts his eyes out. This is a
very important symbolic act—"self-blinding" is literally
what people do when they have profound inner con-
flicts. They blind themselves so that they are closed off in
greater or lesser degree from the reality around them. Since
Oedipus does this after learning how he has been living a
delusion, we may take it as an act symbolizing the tragic
difficulty, the "finiteness" and "blindness" of man in seeing
the truth about himself and his origin.[1]

Even though it was Eve who took the first bite of
the fruit of the tree of knowledge, men have seemed more
bent on the search for truth about life than have women.
Abraham Maslow in *Toward a Psychology of Being* writes,

Many brilliant women are caught up in the problem of
making an unconscious identity between intelligence and
masculinity. To probe, to search, to be curious, to affirm,
to discover, all these she may feel as defeminizing, es-

pecially if her husband in his uncertain masculinity is threatened thereby. Many cultures and many religions have kept women from knowing and studying, and I feel that one dynamic root of this action is the desire to keep them "feminine" (in a sado-masochistic sense); for instance, women cannot be priests or rabbis.[2]

These patterns of keeping women from "knowing" are being broken down in the church and in other institutions. A willingness to look at life truthfully is the basis for much of the feminist argument. If women have not always searched diligently for the truth, they have seemed to know intuitively what was right and what was wrong with their lives.

An awareness of the polarities that exist in life adds a dimension of depth and richness to individual personality that enables one to finally experience the truly joyous and creative life. Between the polarities of life and death, love and hate, joy and sorrow, beauty and ugliness, are a whole variety of tensions, and it is the dealing with these tensions that makes our existence exciting and adds substance to it.

We have just experienced another exquisite Indiana autumn; the foliage has never been more breathtaking, and the "blue October" days seem almost unreal, so bountiful is the beauty of gold and red leaves, of the sunlight shimmering through them. But in the midst of this beauty, the reality is that death is approaching and thus the fall has about it a certain poignant quality that is a part of its truth. An additional part of the truth of this sorrowful season is that the very death that surrounds us in the dying foliage and flowers, is preparation for the life that will burst forth in the spring. We are reminded daily that "in the midst of life we are in death," and that also the converse is true, in the midst of death we are in life. To recognize these poles of existence and the tensions that separate them is all a part of the acceptance of life and of self.

For a truly intimate experience with another person, one has to face the reality that there is an opposite to love and that opposite could be hate, which is an active and aggressive force, or it could be apathy, which connotates indifference and boredom.

In the truly intimate relationship, a woman must come to terms with the possibilities of hostility and aggression when people are living in close, loving relationships. To be unrealistic about the reverse side of the coin of love deprives one in a real sense of the depths of intimacy that can be reached when couples face the truth about themselves and about each other. And the truth is often revealed when hostility opens one to the freedom of leveling with a partner. Dr. George R. Bach, a noted psychologist has recently written a book entitled *The Intimate Enemy*, a book with the provocative subtitle, *How to Fight Fair in Love and Marriage*. In the opening chapter, Dr. Bach maintains that when couples face the reality of the love-hate tensions in marriage and learn to fight fair in an effort to resolve these tensions, a number of benefits accrue to the partnership.

He says:

When our trainees fight according to our flexible system of rules, they find that the natural tensions and frustrations of two people living together can be greatly reduced. Since they live with fewer lies and inhibitions and have discarded out-moded notions of etiquette, these couples are free to grow emotionally, to become more productive and more creative as individuals in their own rights and also as pairs. Their sex lives tend to improve. They are likely to do a better job of raising their children. They feel less guilty about hostile emotions that they harbor against each other. Their communications improve, and as a result, they face fewer unpleasant surprises from their partners. Our graduates know how to make the here-and-now more liveable for themselves, and so they worry much less about the past that cannot be changed. They are less likely to become victims of boredom or divorce. They feel less vulnerable and more loving toward each other because they are protected by an umbrella of reasonable standards for what is fair and foul in their relationship. Perhaps, best of all, they are liberated to be themselves.[3]

The truth does set one free, and the truth is that love does not exist in a vacuum but is a counterpart of aggressive forces that are active in humanity. To face this kind of truth about ourselves and others exacts a price, but when one is willing to pay the price, one gains inestimably in freedom for personal growth.

The person who is truly joyous is deeply aware of the tragic dimensions of life. One cannot experience the ultimate joy of life without having gone through the fire that tempers and strengthens. The pain associated with childbirth is usually transcended by the joyful experience of creation. One thinks of Rose Kennedy and the continuing escalation of tragic events she has faced in her life. Yet her courageous and joyful spirit is an inspiration to all, and her acceptance of life with all of its polarities, is a reminder that sorrow is balanced by joys.

Our greatest literature, which is the cache for the universal wisdom we all share, has usually sprung from tragic events. In 1966 the Nobel prize for literature was given to Nelly Sachs, a German poet who fled to Sweden as the

Nazis rose to power in 1940. Everything—her family, her possessions had been removed from her and she was left, as she attested, "with only a language." Her book O, Ye Chimneys is a poetic testimony that stands parallel to the dumfounding horror and the documentary reports of the Final Solution in the death camps. Her willingness to face and deal with the awful truth of the genocide of her people enabled her to transcend the tragedy through the creation of her poignant and passionate poetry.

It takes a great deal of courage to see the truth about life in general and ourselves in particular. But human beings are so constructed that in greater or lesser degrees they have a desire to see reality as it actually is—even though reality can be terribly painful. Rollo May in interpreting Nietzsche's proclamation, "Error is cowardice!" says: "The reason we do not see the truth is not that we have not read enough books, or do not have enough academic degrees, but that we do not have enough courage."[4]

The search for truth is a part of the inborn capacity for self-awareness, and must be developed if a person is to fulfill himself as a human being.

Jesus said, "Ye shall know the truth, and the truth shall make you free." A freedom of spirit and personality accrues to the woman who is willing to have the courageous heart for truth, and to see her own reality and the reality of the world in dimensions of joy and tragedy.

CHAPTER NINE

Between Him and Me

It doesn't much signify whom one marries, for one is
sure to find next morning that it was someone else.
—SAMUEL ROGERS, *Table Talk*

I was coming out of a theater a short time ago, after
having seen the film *Love Story*. *Love Story* by Erich
Segal is a slim little tale about a Radcliffe girl and a
Harvard boy of different ethnic backgrounds who fall in
love and marry. The girl, Jenny, works very hard to support Oliver, who has alienated his super-rich parents by
his marriage, so he can get through law school. When he
is finished they move to New York; he is taken into an
especially successful law firm; and they begin to enjoy
the rewards of a Harvard law degree. At this point Jenny
dies of leukemia. It is a touching story about Oliver's
love for Jenny, and Jenny's love for Oliver.

As I was leaving the theater, I heard one high school
girl say to another, "Can you imagine anyone ever loving
you that much?" Her friend replied, "Well, I think I
could." The first girl said rather defiantly, "Well, I can't.

I'm sure no one will ever love me like that. And I don't think I could love anyone that much either."

I found this little exchange interesting and rather heart-breaking. I am enough of a romantic to hope that every-one loves someone grandly and completely once in their lives, and that the quality of their love is returned to them.

In spite of the ominous headlines we read, such as "Is the American Family Obsolete?" marriages are still taking place with an unrelenting regularity. The society pages are flourishing with pictures of the bride and the ac-companying standardized report of that high sacrament, the wedding. While the prophets of doom see the family as obsolete, monogamy as overrated, and childlessness the approaching norm, probably love and marriage will prevail. To be sure, some things are happening that can only result in changes in family structure, but whatever happens, one man and one woman will still relate to each other in a comparable situation that marriage involves.

The taking of the marriage vows is an awesome mo-ment, when one considers how completely one entrusts one's life to another. I have advised my daughters not to get married until they have to. By that I mean that they should not consider marriage until they love someone so completely that they can "do no other" thing—that they lit-erally "have to" enter into the marital relationship as the only response to the overwhelming nature of the love they feel for someone else.

The American concept of courtship and the romantic aura embellishing the experiences of the young in our so-ciety are not adequate preparations for the rigors of mar-riage. I recall a long time ago reading of an experiment in which monkeys were enticed through a maze by the sight and smell of bananas. However, when they completed the maze they were given lettuce instead of bananas. Whoever reported this incident compared it to the enticement of the courtship practices in this country, urging the young girl on to a situation that will be prosaic and commonplace instead of heady and exciting as she had been led to believe.

Marriage begins as a "peak experience." The wedding ceremony, the grandly passionate honeymoon, and the joy of establishing a "place" together all contribute to starting the adventure of marriage at the top of the mountain. That is all well and good, providing that the rest of the journey is not all downhill. The marital setting is fraught with pitfalls in which a woman might lose her own identity. Giving up her name is only one in a series of steps in which she could become, as someone has said, "an apostrophe—my husband's wife, my child's mother." But if a woman can bring to her marriage some surety of self, she can avoid the obvious pitfalls and remain her own person, even though she will play various roles within the marital context.

At the moment the marriage vows are spoken, there begins a period of adjustment—it begins, but as far as I can tell at this point in my own marriage, it doesn't end. When two people hopefully decide to become one, there is a never-ending interaction that is set into motion that calls on one daily for decisions and judgments which affect not only the person making them but the partner involved.

In the early months and even years of marriage there is the simple routine of "getting to know you." I can recall hearing my grandmother say, "You have to summer and winter with a man before you really know him." I can accept that homily after twenty-four years of marriage. The existentialist question would be, Do we ever really know another person? Because of the intricacy and complexity of personality, the privateness of "self," it is probably not possible to "know" all about people that we think we do. I think it is healthy and stimulating in marriage for one not to assume that one knows her partner completely; there ought to be some margin for mystery even between personalities that daily confront each other.

Having made the commitment to marriage, one is reminded daily that this was a commitment to the "long haul," that the words of the vows, "in sickness and in health, for richer and for poorer," were not just empty sounds. The reality of what marriage is begins to seep in as responsibilities mount and a couple moves off the top of the mountain.

The kind of attitude assumed early in marriage toward the basic relationship either supports or negates the whole cosmos in which the marriage exists. If a woman approaches this fact of her life with the sense that her marriage is a creative, vital, ever-changing alliance, then she has avoided one of the common pitfalls. There is no danger more threatening to a marriage than the attitude that this situation is static. A headline on a current woman's magazine posed the innocuous question, "Are You Still the Girl Your Husband Married?" and my answer was, "Good grief, I hope not!" If almost a quarter of a century had gone by and I still looked and acted the same, something would be terribly out of whack. What would be even worse than looking like I did twenty-five years ago (although I will admit that was better), would be thinking like I did twenty-five years ago.

It is interesting to me that such a question would be asked. But in our youth-oriented culture, a dubious goal is to remain the same. It is no secret that some men cherish the "little girl" image of their wives and feel more comfortable if she doesn't exhibit signs of growth toward being a more complete and self-sufficient person.

Every stage of marriage exacts change and permits growth if one is wise enough to see what is being called for. In the early stages of marriage a husband and wife can relate to each other strictly as lovers, but the time comes when other roles are added. The presence of children makes parents out of lovers, and the care and attention they demand create a new area of life and growth together. The whole arena of family life presents us with the need to play different roles at different times. We have all been lovers, friends, mothers, nurses, and confidantes to our husbands. It is to this constant role-changing that we committed ourselves in marriage.

In Eric Berne's book *Games People Play* he assigns to people a trilogy of identities; he says that each of us have within us a parent, an adult and a child, and that in varying situations we choose to use the identity that will both give and gain the response we desire.

Part of our responsibility in marriage is to sort out these varying identities and be able to recognize them in both ourselves and our mates. I presume it is the "child" still residing in the American male that lures him to the "game," that sets him in front of the TV for untold hours to watch the "child" in other men scramble for the ball. This kind of behavior often brings out the "parent" in the wife who proceeds to chastise and make value judgments in regard not only to the husbands use of time, but also to his lack of response to her at such times. While the knowledge of this triple identity may not ease the chagrin women feel, it does throw some light on certain behavior patterns. In other situations, such as impulsive buying, the wife's "child" may assert itself, and often in a marriage the two partners may be dealing with each other child to child, rather than adult to adult.

Although there is an alarming divorce rate in this country, when one contemplates the realities of married life, I think it quite remarkable that people do as well as they do. Daily I see evidences of people who have remained "in love," who are happy in the arrangement, and could think of no viable alternative in which they could find equal fulfillment.

The commitment is a two-way street. While the woman commits herself to a life of nurturing and "doing" for others, stringent demands are made upon the male. The responsibility of support can hardly be understated in our materialistic society. In our new move for freedom and rights, it occurs to me that the demands on a woman are greater than ever before.

One of the myths concerning women in our society is that they must be all things to all people. A woman today is expected to be an ideal mate and companion for her husband. She is expected to keep house at least as well as the hirelings in the TV ads do. She is expected to be a lovely hostess and a nearly ideal mother. Along with this she is expected to have time for worthwhile outside interests in the church and community. This high level of performance that is expected and sometimes exacted from a woman takes its toll of her personhood. Frantically trying to be what everyone else expects her to be leaves her little time or motivation to be what she wants to be.

The nature of our economy is such that many women have to work. Many others work because they want to make use of their educated potentials and are challenged in the working situation. This adds new dimensions to the woman's role in marriage and to her relationship with her husband and children.

The working woman may be removed from the scene of housekeeping, but it remains for her to do or to see that it is done by someone. While her work may be challenging, she faces new problems, such as who will care for the children, who will see to it that the shirts are ironed and that meals are prepared. Along with the mundane housekeeping chores, problems of a different nature confront her. She is often besieged by guilt. Questions arise in her own mind as to whether or not the children are deprived because of her absence. She must weigh whether quantity or quality of time spent with them is important. Questions also arise concerning her relationship with her husband when she is operating primarily outside the home. Does it negate him, does it change the quality of their relationship for her to be more sufficient in the working role. Each couple must answer such questions that are posed in a way that makes sense to them. My point simply is that every extension of the woman's role in marriage adds a new set of problems with which she must deal.

The American couple is, as a rule, a very busy couple. They are goal-oriented, always looking toward the goal of a new room on the house, Johnny's college education, a boat, or a trip. One of the results of this "busyness" with things is that the spirit of the marriage may be endangered. A couple may be so engrossed in goals that they are truly unaware of what is happening in their relationship.

I believe it is a woman's responsibility in marriage to keep the relationship between her and her husband center-stage. The high divorce rate occurring after twenty years of what was thought to be a good marriage indicates that a couple were not looking very closely at each other. The children leave home and the adults are each face to face with a stranger. The central task in marriage is for a couple to keep from becoming strangers. The intimate

climate in which marriage flourishes must be kept alive by
mutual concern and communication. What is most needed
for the intimacy to grow is for couples to pay attention to
each other. In the settling years of marriage a husband and
wife can become easily distracted from one another by
the needs of children and by the urgency of "making it"
in this world. These distractions can lead to a pseudo-inti-
macy and a pseudo-communication that bypasses the most
obvious need in a couple's relationship—the need to relate
to each other intimately and honestly and lovingly. If we
pay close enough attention to our mates, our marital radar
picks up signals of various kinds of needs and we can give
the proper response. But if we don't pay attention, and
needs keep going unmet, then the relationship begins to
break down and intimates become strangers.

The hub of a marriage is the personal relationship between two people. The children, the in-laws, the properties
and possessions and vocation are really extraneous to this
basic unit. When a couple fall deeply enough in love that
marriage is the only solution, then they should be willing
to nurture that love, to give it first place in life, and to
build a rewarding relationship upon it that can last till
"death do us part."

CHAPTER TEN

Between Me and Them

> I tell you there's a wall ten feet thick and ten miles
> high between parent and child.
> —G. B. SHAW, *Misalliance*

On the cover of *Look* magazine for September 22, 1970, was the headline, "The Motherhood Myth," followed by a dubious quote, "Women don't need to be mothers any more than they need spaghetti." In the ensuing article there was documentation from doctors and psychologists that motherhood is not instinctual, that marriages without children are happier than marriages with children, and that, generally speaking, having and raising children is never worth the price exacted for this completely human enterprise.

In the same month, appearing in *Redbook* magazine was a taped interview in which Dr. Masters of the famous Masters and Johnson duet, was reported as saying,

Somewhere along the line, Mother Nature talks to every female. There is, I'm convinced, an innate female demand to reproduce. It's real; it's a tremendous instinct. It's not too much of a factor for many women when they are twenty-three, twenty-four—but when thirty-three or thirty-four rolls around, the gal looks in the mirror and says, "Well, how much time do I have, oh Lord?"[1]

In spite of the documentation that Betty Rollins avows in the article in *Look* magazine, it seems that Dr. Masters is closer to the zone of truth that most women feel about themselves. The physical capacity to bear children and the psychological need to be in the nurturant role seem basic to the feminine instinct. While it is true that momentous changes are being effected in the family structure, and that woman will be freer than ever not to bear children, it boggles the mind to consider a civilization that turns its back on motherhood and parenthood. The fact is that people and societies change very slowly. George Gallup, Jr., the pollster, has pointed out that "even the most unsettling trends that emerged in the 60's and 70's are evolutionary rather than revolutionary."[2]

Most women in our culture will give birth to one or more children, and for over two-thirds of their life span will find themselves in the role of mother. A key to the woman's identity will be found in this relationship—not that she necessarily lives vicariously through her children, but that the fact of what is happening between her and them adds to her measure of self.

From one point of view, child raising is the same as it has been through countless generations of civilization. Max Coots suggests this in *The National Observer*. He continues:

As the first teachers of language, parents give the child his mother tongue with which he progressively learns to think and feel. Language is basic to the total personality development of an individual, and because language is seldom neutral it is the major way that parents transmit and reinforce the fears, hopes, values, taboos, and customs of both the family and the culture. This has not changed.

From another point of view, however, child raising has changed drastically in recent decades. The home, once the most central of all institutions in American society, no longer can claim that unique centrality. For good and bad, the home has had its traditional functions reduced or diluted by having to share its functions with other institutions and with external social forces.[3]

Someone has said, "There is no man, had he been born ten years earlier or ten years later than he was who would not have been a different man." Thus it is that our lives are shaped in part by the common pressures exerted on us by the society and culture in which our time is cast. Our concern is not only that children live in the rapidly changing maelstrom that is today's society; it is rather that parents must operate in this upheaval and still manage somehow to provide the value training that has been their responsibility since men and women have lived in family units.

An interesting development in our country which has occurred in the two decades following the Second World War has been the child-centered culture. More families were established in 1946 than had ever been established in the history of our nation. (The number of families established in 1946 was record-breaking, and not matched or surpassed in number until 1968, when an estimated 2,100,000 marriages occurred. These two booms were related: The 1968 figure reflects the large number of children from the postwar family boom.) These statistics were reported in *The National Observer*, February 2, 1970.

This postwar situation followed three decades of unusual upheaval in our nation; the shattering social force of the twenties, the great depression of the thirties, and the all-consuming war effort of the forties. Women, after several war years, which took many of them out of the home and into factories and stores, rushed back to a home base and begat children with a vengeance.

For the first time in our society's history, conditions were such that parents could focus on their children in a manner that moved sociologists to dub this the "child-centered" society. We had moved steadily away from the rural society that had permeated not only rural America but also small towns. In that society children were of economic benefit, and their journey through childhood was hastened along, because as adults they were of even more economic benefit in the family structure than they were as children.

In the new society, children were costly, but as with all expensive things they were to be savored and enjoyed for themselves. America was growing steadily more affluent, and materialism was becoming a way of life. Surrounded by material blessings that would have been incomprehensible two generations ago, American parents responded by showering their children with a battery of "things" that literally forced the child to cope with a chaotic environment; the simple life has become past history by virtue of the number of "things" with which we and our children must daily contend. The increase of leisure time and the cry for "togetherness" sponsored by *McCall's* magazine and used skillfully by the advertising industry led us into focusing attention on the child in a way that has ultimately appeared to be harmful. It was as if we were satisfying our own needs, rather than actually seeing to the deep needs of children, and this goal, even though it may be an unconscious one, is bound to backfire.

In this child-centered culture we have been engulfed,

as no parents previously have been, with information, advice, and literature from the experts. But reading does not turn us into experts, and while we might have more psychological insight than our parents had, we still must grope and experiment and succeed sometimes and fail sometimes as parents. Our whole attitude toward our responsibility as parents is shifted in a child-centered culture. Jules Henry in *Culture Against Man* says:

> What we see so much in America, then, is that the psychoanalytic metaphor according to which the child introjects the parent (copies the parents, tries to come up to parental expectation) it stood on its head, and the parent copies the child. In America today it is not alone that the child wants to live up to parental expectations, but that the parent wants also—often desperately—to live up to the child's expectations. And just as the traditional child was torn between what he wanted and what his parents wanted, so the contemporary American parent is buffeted between what he thinks he believes to be good for his child and what he thinks he knows would gratify him in relation to his child. In these circumstances, the children themselves tend to become more disoriented. The need to follow the child contributes to the impulses that produce the crewcut on the balding father and, lest we forget, the "accent on youth" in the mother.[4]

Perhaps one of the deepest frustrations that we have as parents is that children seem constitutionally indisposed to profit from someone else's experience. This is why I believe in original sin, because I see daily the human's demand for his own experience to free will, for his own search for identity and integrity as he moves toward maturity. I'm sure this is related to the slow evolvement of societies socially and morally: everyone seemingly starts from scratch. A psychoanalyst wrote that he thought the whole story of the Exodus of the Jews and the passing into the promised land was really the myth of the young person groping toward maturity. While I would not pass off a part of the history of Judaism that lightly, it does seem that growing up is an adventure that all of human history announces you must, in part at least, do by yourself. And yet, we do not really believe that. We strongly believe that children need our help to grow up, and if they seem to deny and resist us, they need more help.

We are parents in an age that is characterized by change —change so rapid and so forceful that all our institutions and values are called into question. Everything in the value system is "up for grabs," and in this chaotic economic-social upheaval we must try to raise our own children to be wholesome adults. In the midst of this panorama of change there are some things that remain constant. One of these constants is that we are not raising children: we are raising adults, guiding persons as they move toward maturity. Another area that has remained constant throughout man's long and troubled pilgrimage on earth is that of his basic needs, both physical and emotional. Regardless of what society is contributing to or inflicting upon our children, there are certain emotional needs that must be met if our children are to reach the ultimate goal of responsible adulthood, with its contingent emotional and spiritual maturity.

One of the most basic and earliest emotional needs of the child is his need for love. Children have built-in radar that picks up the truth about how other people feel about them. They respond to non-verbal signals as well as to verbal allusions to love. They will sense that one loves them if the expression on one's face and the tone of one's voice convey that feeling. My daughter was having difficulty in explaining to me why she did not like a certain teacher, and she finally summed it up eloquently by saying, "Well, when she smiles at me, it's only with her mouth." Love is conveyed by showing interest in things that are important to a child. To enjoy, to laugh, to project yourself back into your own childhood and remember says something important to children concerning the way you feel about them.

Children need to feel that they are capable of achievement. It is important to give children the chance to enjoy their own accomplishments. Mothers who take the bows at recitals and fathers who get patted on the back at Little League are reducing the sense of accomplishment that a child should get from his own achievements. A child needs some tasks he can do readily and some that will challenge his creativity, that help him to stretch and grow. Praise for accomplishments is a bonus to his sense of achievement. Adults often withhold praise, because they equate praise with softness of character. Praise given justly has the opposite effect, because it strengthens one's sense of worth and importance. And all of us need to feel that sense of worth and importance. We can help our children to this end by showing them that we value their opinion and give them consideration. It is one thing to ask for an opinion from a child; it is quite another to act as if that opinion was worthwhile and usable. As we teach our children to relate to others, their own sense of importance is realized. As they come into more and more contact with people, there will be more opportunity for others to enrich them.

This need for confirmation and recognition in children is a very basic need. One of the simplest and most desirable things you can do as a mother to give your child recognition is to look at him when you talk. If it is necessary to get down on your knees to do this, it is worth the effort in meaning conveyed to children. No greater thrill comes to any of us than to know another person recognizes our own special worth.

Never have parents operated more in a vacuum when it comes to guiding a child in his need for help in evaluating behavior. In spite of the loose value system that seems a part of our society, a child still needs to learn socially acceptable behavior. Extreme methods of discipline need to be avoided, and an understanding given to the child concerning why certain behavior is acceptable. Mothers need the insight to look for causes as to why children behave as they do. A full measure of trust in one's children pays striking dividends as they grow in responsibility for their own behavior.

There seems to be much evidence to indicate that children need assurance, that is, they need something in which to believe. Like adults they are moved by the experiences of life which may come to us in the way of family traditions, or the sacraments, or any of those things which have in them "some quality that goes beyond, that transcends the actual thing that is happening." When parents are confused about their own values or belief system, it is very difficult to give children this quality of assurance. When parents are too sure that they have all the answers, children tend to resist this blanket application of a value system.

One evening my daughters and I were ready to go to the airport to pick up my husband who was due in on the evening plane. We received word that his plane had been held up for several hours in Cincinnati and there we were, all dressed up and no place to go. Bunny, a junior in college, suggested brightly that we go see the movie *Rosemary's Baby*. Dawn who was then a junior in high school, chimed in with her support of the idea. "That's a good idea, Mother. You haven't taken us to see a movie in a long time." I declined their suggestion and they were not at all happy at my response. "Why won't you take us?" Bunny asked. I gave a variety of reasons as my rationale for not taking my daughters to see *Rosemary's Baby*. I had read the book, been appalled at the central idea of it, and had felt that I did not care to put my stamp of approval on the kind of movie that seems to be getting more and more popular in this country. I did not want to be the one to take my girls to this particular movie which would lend my support to the philosophy of such undertakings. "But, Mother, that's ridiculous!" said Bunny. "You know Dawn and I will see that show—so why don't you take us?" But I resisted with what I felt was a valid rationale. "I know you'll go," I said, "but not in my presence or with my support. You are old enough to make some value judgments, but so am I. And I choose not to take you to this particular show. Let it be on your own head." This led us into an evening's discussion about the whole matter of a belief system, and what it can mean to the children of a family.

My husband and I are grounded in the Christian faith, and what we have done with our lives has been in a large part motivated by our response to the Christian experience. When I married Blair he was a minister in the Church of the Brethren, and for the past fifteen years he has been president of Manchester College, a denominational college that combines the Christian faith as an integral part of the learning process. I allude to these conditions in our life mainly to indicate that our daughters were raised within a specific belief system. Sunday school and church were a regular part of their growing up, and they were exposed to a variety of religious experiences both inside and outside the home.

But that evening I could not help wondering if we had accomplished anything concerning the spiritual verities of life. In a no-holds-barred conversation they let me know that while they had both joined the church at the prescribed age, they were searching for their own truth. This I could accept, but it was more difficult to accept Bunny's blunt statement, "Your values are not necessarily my values." As a sophisticated college student I knew she had had her share of exposure to some of the truth of life from which her father and I would have liked to have shielded her.

More discussion followed concerning our various opinions of smoking, drinking, using drugs, and sex mores. My daughters informed me in ways from which I could not escape that the three of us were operating on different wave lengths when it came to our values about these things. As the evening was coming to a close, I was beginning to feel that Blair and I had failed completely—that the girls had been more moved by outside pressures than I had realized. In a sort of desperation I asked, "Well, if you don't accept our values and our faith, what have we given you? Do we leave you with no certainties after living with us for twenty-one years?"

They then hastened to assure me that they hadn't said an absolute no to our values and certainly not to the faith. They reserved the right to work things out for themselves. They thought, and I agreed with them, that this was fair as well as inevitable.

After some moments of quiet reflection following the rather heated pace we had been going, Bunny said, "But you did give us something that I feel is very important to both of us." "What was that?" I asked her. She answered, "You gave us a sense of surety about your own beliefs. I've never had doubts as to your and Daddy's real belief in

Christianity and your personal values." Dawn agreed that it was comforting to know one could have a belief system and operate freely within it.

I've thought about that evening's conversation many times and pondered some of the exchange that took place. I've decided that surety is important. Even if our children can't accept our values without question, without their own experimentation, they can still have some assurance from knowing that their parents felt strength and reality in their value system.

That evening was a bridge over the generation gap. I think the generation gap exists in negative ways, but that it can be a positive force in the family situation. I think it is negative when it exists because communication is blocked, because people don't really care enough to find out the causes for a lack of communication. I believe in open hearts and open mouths, in touching and talking, in the inviolate selfhood of each individual in the family, in the assumption of solidarity and support when needed. I believe all these things help close the negative generation gap. But I think the generation gap is a necessity when people are striving for their own identity. People in their late teens need to escape the intimacy that has been foisted upon them so they can grow. I believe in that healthy distance between them and me. They need it for their growth to selfhood, and I need it so I don't rely on them for my identity.

Erik Erikson, a true visionary about childhood and society constructed a ladder of psychological needs that starts with infancy and ends with adulthood. He believed that until a child was five, his most urgent need is love. Between the ages of five and twelve he needs the satisfaction of accomplishment. Identification with others, being part of the crowd, is his chief need between the ages of twelve and sixteen. From sixteen to twenty-one he is searching for intimacy, that relationship of one to one that plays such an important part in our growth. The years between twenty-one and thirty are years of struggle as one reaches for maturity. Above thirty, Erikson feels that the deepest need we have is the need of integrity about our lives—that yearning to be at peace with oneself and one with the universe. I am intrigued that what we really are guiding our children toward is not just maturity, but maturity made richer with a sense of integrity.

I am happy that I can find some of my identity through being a mother, and I would like to think that the mothering sense that being a woman implies does not stop with our own children. There are other people's children who need love and confirmation, there are minority groups that need support and help. There are many ways in which a woman, married or single, is constantly challenged to use the nurturant qualities that are inherent in her identity as a woman.

Our Spiritual Identity

CHAPTER ELEVEN

Awareness of Grace

I come in the little things,
Saith the Lord.
—EVELYN UNDERHILL, *Immanence*

Shortly after we moved to this community, I was called on
at various times to speak before several women's clubs
and different kinds of groups. To simplify things for myself, I devised a speech wherein I put on an assortment of
hats to demonstrate my points. Many of the hats were
facetious and funny, but toward the end of the speech I
began to get quite serious. The last hat I wore was an
old Brethren bonnet which was a striking symbol of
my own heritage. Wearing this quaint black bonnet, I
talked at length about my faith and my belief in a sure
sense of a center of life in God. I was destined to don
those hats several hundred times before a cross section of
midwestern audiences, mainly women, representing a wide
diversity of life styles and belief systems. The thing that
always impressed me, and that moved me to say yes to so
many invitations, was an obvious spiritual hunger that my
listeners inevitably disclosed. Time and again I was

struck by the rapt attention and depth of listening that I was accorded. And when I was through, many women would come to me and in various ways express a deep and unsatisfied longing for the life of the spirit.

At a time when women in our culture are evaluating their situations more carefully than ever, and examining their lives from varying legal and political stances, I feel that some cognizance must be given to the spiritual identity of women. The busyness of their lives, the distractions of their days, the climate of their varying relationships, take on new and deeper meanings when God is at the center of life. Believing that God is the source of all of life, if we are detached or cut loose from the "vital root" of our existence we "flounder in an abyss of meaninglessness." Woman is basically a spiritual being and for a woman to attain wholeness, I feel she must give attention to this spiritual overlay of her existence. She is, after all, a co-creator with God, and in the best sense she cares for what she creates in a way that often transcends human qualities. Even if she does not give birth to a child, she is often in the role of minister to others, and such a role implies the presence of spirituality.

To enter into the life of the spirit, one must first be aware of grace, that movement of God toward us. That is the great fact for which all religion stands—the confrontation of the human soul with God. We are never allowed to live a purely human life with complete peace of mind, because in our restlessness and hunger God is seeking us out.

In myriads of ways, in daily situations, God's grace moves toward us with continual gifts, but many of us choose not to recognize this reality for what it is. If a woman is truly seeking to satisfy her deepest spiritual nature, she will be responsive to and aware of grace in her life. Responding to this awareness leads us to the nurturing and developing of our interior life. If we desire relationship with God, we must be willing to pay attention to Him. Simone Weil calls this the "divine attention," and without this inner discipline of divine attentiveness, our efforts toward interior growth will fail. Thomas Kelly in his *A Testament of Devotion* writes with rare insight into the conditions of this divine attentiveness.

He says,

Deep within us all there is an amazing inner sanctuary of the soul, a holy place, a Divine Center, a speaking Voice, to which we may continuously return. Eternity is at our hearts, pressing upon our time-torn lives, warming us with intimations of an astounding destiny, calling us home unto Itself. Yielding to these persuasions, gladly committing ourselves in body and soul, utterly and completely to the Light Within, is the beginning of true life. It is a dynamic center, a creative Life that presses to birth within us. It is a Light within which illumines the face of God and casts new shadows and new glories upon the face of men. It is a seed stirring to life if we do not choke it. It is the Shekinah of the soul, the Presence in the midst. Here is the Slumbering Christ, stirring to be awakened, to become the soul we clothe in earthly form and action. And He is within us all.[1]

Thomas Kelly and others have shown us that it is possible to live life on two levels. That is, we can go about running our errands, attending to our work, relating to others on one level. But on a deeper level, in that "Shekinah of the soul," we can be attentive to God.

That is the struggle that interior life presents us with, to be in the here and now, doing what we are called upon to do, and yet to be one with God, to be in constant adoration of Him who is the Center of life. For years, the admonishment of Paul, to pray without ceasing, was a puzzle to me. How, I wondered, if one was to get anything at all done in this world, could one be in a constant state of prayer? Who would care for the kiddies, and clean the streets, and who would run the government if we all prayed without ceasing? But when the light came to me, I understood. One can be living at two levels at once, the one level of doing and being, and the other level of prayer and adoration. When Nels Ferré, a famous theologian, and his brother asked his mother how to pray, she answered, "Praise Him and Thank Him, Praise Him and Thank Him." If one learns how to live life on two levels, one is in a constant state of Praising Him and Thanking Him.

Florence Allshorn, an English mystic, learned to live life on this double edge, and whenever she was in conversation with someone, at a deeper level she was praying for him.

The fostering of the interior life leads us inexorably to the life of prayer. As Douglas Steere says,

> There is no record of growth in the interior life in those who do not know prayer. The rule is almost as blunt as that: no prayer, no interior life. And we have no record of a saint who did not pray, or of real growth in the interior life that is not marked by this inner yielding or inner attention to God. For finally He asks for our wills and for the deep intent which is prayer.[2]

When we come to have some understanding of the real depth at which life was meant to be lived, the nature of God's grace becomes clearer to us. In my own spiritual journey I have come to the place where I see God's grace everywhere about me. Sitting at my kitchen window, watching the squirrels and the birds and the little things of the earth, I am filled with the grace of creation. Their innocence and trust and beauty move me to thank Him for His creatures. And watching the tall oak trees bend and sway in the wind, I wonder if we are not in Paradise yet, but have not enough light to see the world as it truly is. Watching other people's children, the grace and beauty with which they move fills me with thankfulness, and I wonder how anyone can look at these children of God and not respond to something that goes beyond all humanness. In constant ways, the grace of God comes to me, in conversations with friends which have the dimensions of that second level of life, though all we are saying to each other are prosaic and daily things. In chance conversations, some new light is given to me, and it is as if God were whispering the truth through that person confronting me. In the family situation there are daily expressions of God's grace as individuals relate in the most intimate experience that human life affords us.

Florence Allshorn reminds us often that God uses ordinary people in extraordinary ways. When that happens the grace of God flows through the person being used; one is literally a channel of His love.

At different times in my life I have been on the receiving end of such expressions of grace. I have had on several occasions what Douglas Steere refers to as the "Grand Canyon experience of the soul, where one is opened deep and the winds of God blow through one at will." Often in my deepest moments of struggle some person has said that thing or suggested some reading, or has done something that has made all the difference. I am willing to call that grace. I think I have been used by God on different occasions, and I am willing and thankful if I can be a channel of grace.

Several years ago it was necessary for me to be hospitalized for a rather routine checkup. Knowing I would be there for several days, I packed up a few of my favorite books, and some new ones I had intended to read and prepared myself for a time of silence and solitude. I had asked for and been assured a private room, intending to study and possibly write, and while I didn't long to be hospitalized, I rather looked forward to some time alone. I was disappointed on my arrival early one evening to discover I was to share a room with someone else. When I entered the room a rather young and attractive woman was pacing the floor and moaning. She obviously was not pleased to see me, and she said in a sullen voice that I would just have to be able to stand her moaning and groaning. I assured her I could, and I unpacked, trying to be very private and contained in my half of the room. As the evening wore on it was obvious she was not going to communicate with me, and I, feeling a little put upon, was also very quiet.

After breakfast was over the next morning a young doctor came in to see my roommate, pulled the curtain between our beds, and announced in a rather loud voice that the liver scan was positive and that she had only a couple of months to live. I lay there rather stunned and wondered how I would have felt if my approaching death had been announced to me in such an offhand manner. When the doctor left the room, we were engulfed in a terrible silence that was only broken by the appearance of nurses and doctors. I prayed that I might be sensitive enough not to do or say anything that would cause the strange woman lying next to me any more pain than she was already enduring.

Later that afternoon when we were alone and very quiet, she said simply, "You heard!" There followed an experience of days of fellowship and friendship that I have always treasured. She was curious about all the books I had with me, and when she saw that most of them were about the spiritual life, she began to question me at length about my faith, my faith in God and in the spirit of man. One morning she sat up in bed and said, "Pat, you were sent here to be with me this week. For a long time I've wanted to talk to someone about the things of the spirit, and I've never even had the courage to speak to the minister. I've gone to church, but there were no answers. You and your books were sent here." Then she had a strange request. Would I, she wondered, help her prepare her funeral service. Together we searched the Scriptures and the writings of the saints to find what most expressed her and seemed most relevant to her. I wheeled her down to the fourth floor, and we sat there in the hospital chapel, the stained glass throwing colored shadows on our faces, and we explored the hymnal for the best expressions of her renewed faith and spirit. We visited at length about many things, and we laughed together over the vicissitudes of hospital life. Then she would say reflectively, "I'm laughing—can you believe that I'm laughing?"

People came and went; we shared our family and friends with each other briefly. We lit a multicolored candle in our window and marveled at the beauty of the flickering colors on our wall. One evening after a day which had been fruitful and pleasant together, she said, "I'm grateful to have had this delightful day." I watched her spirit unfold in preparation for the Via Dolorosa that lay ahead of her, and I was grateful to be the witness of such valiant courage.

She left the hospital before I did, for a few weeks respite before she was brought back to die. Her parting words as she squeezed my hand were, "Hasn't this week been something?" It is something when we are aware that even in our ordinariness we can be used in an extraordinary way. It is something when the recipient of God's grace recognizes it for what it is and isn't afraid to call it by the right name. It is something when God sets two strangers down together for a few days and lets His love weave back and forth between the yearnings and deepest needs of their hearts.

The natural response to God's grace is gratitude, and a person who finds herself aware of this grace will be in a constant attitude of prayer. This is the crux of the matter. As one evolves in one's discipline of the interior life, everything is put into a new perspective. Some things that seemed so important to us become minimized, and this sense of detachment gives us a new freedom. Other things suddenly become glaringly important as our life and relationships come under the "scrutiny of that Light within," which is a daily confrontation with God.

D. H. Lawrence says there are three kinds of people in the world. There are those who have seen the Light, and who are an authentic channel of God's grace and love on earth. There are those who have not had direct access, but who are willing to reflect the Light that someone else has given them. And there are those who are not aware that there is a Light.

Douglas Steere tells of an old Muslim who declared, "The true saint goes in and out amongst the people and eats and sleeps with them and buys and sells in the market and marries and takes part in social intercourse and never forgets God for a single moment."

That is how woman may yet find her true identity, to go about doing her work, whatever that work might be, doing all the things that seem normal and right, nurturing her husband and children, and in the midst of all the busyness to be overwhelmingly conscious of God, who is the root of her being, and in whom wholeness and completeness reside.

CHAPTER TWELVE

Shedding the Mantle of Self

I hope all goes well with you. It will when the "I" is
taken out. Not till then.

—Florence Allshorn

Meister Eckhart wrote: "There are plenty to follow our
Lord half-way, but not the other half. They will give up
possessions, friends and honors, but it touches them too
closely to disown themselves." The nurture and development of the interior life leads us in a specific direction.
Finally it brings us face to face with ourselves and reveals
the deep recesses of selfishness that are part of all of us.
We know that heroic lives have been lived by men and
women who were able to liberate their egos, but the way
seems unattainable, almost harsh. Living as we do en-
meshed and engrossed in a world of things makes selfishness seem a part of the system. In a society where one
must promote oneself to get ahead, to get one's share of
the things, it seems almost ridiculous to talk about giving
up self. And yet that is what we are called to do, if we
would live a free and creative life.

If there is one directive that we get with a surety from

the pages of the New Testament, it is that "he who would find his life must lose it." In different settings and in different ways Christ reminded the disciples and others who followed Him that the way to the abundant life was through the giving up of self.

This is one of the most difficult ways to choose to live, and for Christ this life style led him unwaveringly to the cross. Christ had a self to give—no man ever lived with a surer sense of identity than Christ. He knew himself, and He understood the purpose of His life.

We are not Christs and we will not be called upon to go the way of the cross, but for the truly joyous life we must be able to shed the mantle of self. Like Christ, we must be sure of self before trying to give up "self."

Florence Allshorn said, "I came to know myself so well, I could forget myself completely." What I am talking about is a joyous abandonment of self, not a martyred existence that is a poor substitute for the real thing.

When we moved from a city parish to our little town, and my husband became a college president, our lives were altered greatly. As a minister, Blair's office had been in the church which was next door to the parsonage, and we had a lot of "togetherness" going. I was deeply involved with the members of our church. I went with Blair to do some of the calling, and in many other ways I was closely concerned with his ministry. He was "at hand" through the proximity of his office and the nature of his work, and our family had grown very used to a way of life where we were really "together."

After the move to Manchester, I was very much on the periphery of Blair's life. His new job took concentrated attention and occupied most of his waking hours. He was seldom home for meals, even if he happened to be in town, but he often traveled away from home base a good part of the time, and he was simply no longer available to us in the way he had been. I suddenly felt abandoned; my intimate involvement in his work was no longer necessary, nor even advisable. I felt very sorry for myself and for the two little girls who had been used to a daddy who had taken them to the park almost daily, and had usually been around at bedtime.

This self-pity grew in the soil of frustration and it showered out on all the rest of the family. I was irritable and seemed to lack any understanding of what I was doing to the people around me. The girls were picking up the tensions that filled our household and the whole nature of our family situation was steadily worsening.

One morning when I was feeling particularly put upon, a letter came from a friend saying that she was sending me a book that had been meaningful to her, and she hoped I would find it so. I have always felt that this was the grace of God working through my friend, because her gift opened my eyes to my own selfishness and led me into a deeper understanding of the Christian way of life.

The book was a biography of a rather obscure English woman, Florence Allshorn, who believed and committed herself to the belief that one could live by the two great commandments, Thou shalt love thy God with all thy heart, soul and mind, and Thou shalt love thy neighbor as thyself.

Believing utterly in her mission, she founded St. Julian's community wherein people lived according to these laws of love. The founding of St. Julian's was the apex of her Christian career, which had begun as a social worker and a missionary in Uganda and had advanced to her being the chief administrator and teacher in a college that prepared young missionaries for their work abroad.

But it was the personality of Florence Allshorn, her willingness to let go of self, and her insight into the deep needs of the people around her, that caught my imagination.

At a time when I was preoccupied with myself, my little hurts, my feelings, her writing came into my vision as if it were heaven-sent to me to show me the littleness, the brokenness of life when one concentrates on self. She wrote in a letter to a good friend,

> It is only as we vow ourselves to obedience that we begin to see that we, as we are, can never enter this fresh, free, utterly lovely Kingdom of heavenly love. That takes us a long time because of the "I" ingrained in every beat of our hearts, every moment of our minds, every habit of our habitual days;—slowly, by determined will, we have to empty ourselves. When humility is there we start really following, but not before. It is the first obedience; to disobey the order to be humble turns us into Pharisees, hypocrites, and pious prigs.
>
> I hope all goes well with you. It will when the "I" is taken out. Not till then. When you really see that so deeply that you are acting a little on it, you wonder why on earth you clung to that little puffed-up being so long. The release and clearness of the joy is so different and the peace at the center of you.[1]

I took the message of this letter as if it were written purposefully for me, and I began to experience the release and joy about which Allshorn writes. I began, through the reading of this book, to see the truth about myself, and the truth was not pleasant to see. I finally recognized that if our home was to be the joy-filled place that it had once been, that I would be the key person in bringing about a change. I realized that Blair had never needed more from me, and that I had never given less. I knew that the girls absorbed attitudes like little sponges and when my attitudes began to change, they trotted willingly along and changed with me.

Allshorn said, "What is important is not how others affect me, but how I affect others." I thought of Blair and his new hard work, and how I had been affecting him. When he needed my understanding and love, I had been so full of self that I could give only bitterness and bickering. When he needed to come home to quietness, he had come home to demands. Little by little the healing process began—as the "mantle of self" began to lift slowly, slowly.

When Blair came home tired and upset, I responded with love. And the love seemed to act as a refresher that washed away his own bitterness. I helped the girls to see reasons that he had to leave us so much, that his service to others enhanced our lives, and that we paid a small price for getting to help build a dream.

I look back on my "period of adjustment" to this situation as one of the times in my life when I made the "leap of faith," when I reached a little higher than I had before, when spiritual truths became more of a reality in my life than they had ever been. I do not mean to imply that I had "arrived," because in the life of the spirit it is the "journey, not the arrival," that matters. But I felt I was moving again toward a goal and that movement forward made a great deal of difference.

I have had the privilege of knowing several women who have truly gotten rid of the "mantle of self." In each case, these women have very strong identities, and much of their identity comes from a deep spiritual attunement to life, a Christ-centeredness which they consciously sought. Two of them have lived in the shadows of their husbands' greatness, but they were absolutely necessary and willing instruments for this greatness to have manifested itself. All of them share their wisdom and joy in the spirit.

I am not advocating that women can serve only in someone's shadow. Whatever a woman does, whether she commits herself to a cause outside her normal pursuits, or to a job, true greatness of soul and spirit is attained only through selflessness. I would not wish to minimize the difficulty of attaining to this virtue. I think if we can only experience moments of selflessness, then we begin to understand the creative rush of the spirit that accompanies a totally selfless action. One begins with the obvious selfishness that is part of being human. Then one goes a little deeper to find the subtle ways we promote self, often at the expense of someone else. Slowly, the mantle lifts, and the creative and joyous life that follows helps us to understand Tertullian's declaration, "The Christian saint is hilarious."

The reward of this selflessness is a marvelous sense of freedom, because the more of self we can let go, the less vulnerable we are to the various threats imposed upon us by society and by individuals. Will Durant, in the opening of his great *History of Civilization*, says, "No one is born into this world, in any culture or society without chains." Women sometimes feel their chains are too heavy to bear, and something drastic must be done about this; but no chains are as binding as the chains of self. The enemy from within is as malicious as the enemy from without.

No job, no career, no creative attainment in the arts, brings the attendant freedom that comes to life when one takes Christ's directive concerning "self" seriously. Florence Allshorn writes,

Anyone who has known the release which comes from the death of self and the inflow of spiritual power which follows, knows that this is a real experience. What follows is always a little more light, so that God and not self is glorified in heart and mind.[2]

This kind of release makes it possible for a woman to fulfill a great part of her reason for being. Women were made to love, and as they move forward in their spiritual growth, an attendant benefit seems to be an increased capacity for loving. Not only the quantity is altered, but more significantly the quality of their love assumes new and deeper dimensions, which enhance all the relationships in which they find themselves.

It is interesting to me that women are thought of as passive beings, and also the ones who especially guard and nurture the precious emotion of love. For love is not a passive element in our lives. It is an active, seeking, searching, doing quality, and one who is truly engaged in the act of loving is not being passive.

Erich Fromm says,

Beyond the element of giving, the active character of love becomes evident in the fact that it always implies certain basic elements, common to all forms of love. These are care, responsibility, respect, and knowledge.[3]

In our society there is a great tendency to exploit others by reducing persons to the status of things. We turn people into things when we value and deal with them only in terms of their function as well as their usefulness to us. The quality of love that the Greek word *eros* implies is this kind of love. We love because it will do us some good, it will be ego building or pleasure giving as it is returned to us. Or we love extensions of ourselves or other loved ones, because we see an object already loved in these extensions. It is not difficult to love a smaller image of ourselves.

Eros has in it the quality of acquisitiveness—we search to find objects worthy enough of our love. We look for value in objects such as looks, character, temperament, social standing, and various other assessments of persons to see if they are worthy of the love which we might bestow. Many basic family problems arise when parents withhold love from a child they somehow deem unworthy. Maybe they are unattractive, or they don't come up to family standards in terms of accomplishment, and therefore love is withheld from them. This is often a subtle and unconscious thing, but it happens. Whole races are sometimes categorized as unworthy of love, beneath the realm of others' consideration and appreciation, not because they are truly unworthy, but because the quality of people's love is often of a limited nature, and is not inclusive of all of God's children.

But when one is able to shed the "mantle of self," whole new possibilities of love are open to them. A woman who has begun to get rid of self has a freedom to respond to others that she has never had before. In *An Inward Legacy* Forbes Robinson writes,

> I have more and more come to the conclusion for some time past that the only reality underlying and explaining the world must be personal. I know that I am a person and that it is persons—especially a few particular persons—not things, who have influenced me and had a power in my life. All my ideas of justice and purity and goodness are inseparably bound up with persons. At last I have come to the conclusion that nothing exists except the personal, and that below all is One who is personal.[4]

I agree with Robinson, and it is this deeply personal element in life that weights our responses to others with such importance. In the New Testament Paul introduces us to a different kind of love, *agape*, which is an outflow of Divine love, a love that descends from God and is in itself an act of grace. It is the kind of love that Paul is writing about in the thirteenth chapter of I Corinthians. It has in it a selfless and disinterested quality, and it does not look for value in return for love given.

Because of God's goodness, it is possible for human beings to move forward spiritually and to invest their relationships with *agape* love.

The woman who is able to love in this dimension is able to accept people as they are. No thought is more comforting than the thought that we are acceptable, just as we are. To think of having to change constantly in order to please the people around us gives rise to all kinds of frustration and bitterness. Jesus accepted people as they were, and this very acceptance led others to scoff at Him. He was not picky and choosy about his neighbors; He was quite free to associate with those whose company was avoided by respectable people. It is this quality of acceptance that makes such a difference in a woman's life. If she can accept the people around her, with their foibles and their shortcomings, she adds to their feelings of worth and promotes their growth into "humanness." If she is accepting, it relieves her of a great deal of strain, because acceptance removes the need for making constant demands on others.

When a woman's love has in it this added dimension of God's love she is able to respond to others with her whole being and not just a part of herself. That is why she invariably draws others to her. There is great satisfaction in knowing that someone is giving us their complete attention. In a world where the impersonal abounds, to be confronted by one who is truly interested in us, who is present, and not "running off on errands" as someone has suggested, is an experience of love. If a woman can permeate the "place" with this sensitivity of the needs of others, she makes an immeasurable contribution to the quality of the lives within her family circle.

Agape love sharpens one's eyesight. People who love others with this total abandonment of self, see others in a different light. They see past the "objectness" of persons, into the deep spirit of life. Allshorn saw others, not in their littleness and imperfection, but she saw others as "God intended them to be." Jesus saw others with an unrelenting clarity, but what He saw did not shake Him up, because His deep love enabled Him to see into the potentials and possibilities of others. His love gave them worth; He didn't seek for value but bestowed value on others.

The problem with which we are faced is whether or not we can love as Christ loved. This seems to be the great adventure a person sets himself upon when one recognizes God's grace working in his life and struggles to let go of self. Allshorn suggested it was the "contemplation of Jesus that would make possible the kind of love He demanded." She writes:

> If I have any advice to give at all, I would beg you to study Jesus Christ in His dealings with men, until the stand He takes every time glows and burns within your hearts, so that you yourselves can do no other when the same things happen to you. And I would beg you to pray that you may learn to love as Jesus Christ loved, with

more passion and with more insistency than anything you have ever prayed for in your life, and then refuse defeat. Perhaps you will be able to do no more, but refuse defeat.[5]

This kind of love demands growth, a continual reaching for what we thought was beyond us, a continual quest that makes us go down deeper than we had intended to or wanted to. If we are created by God's love and He is love, then it follows that our real calling in life is to learn to love fully and completely in His spirit.

Love, if it is worth giving to one, is worth giving to all. We are not called just to love our husbands or our children. If we learn to love in Christ's spirit, then our love will be inclusive of all of humanity. Every child will be our child, and every person will be important and unique. It is this kind of love that calls people out of themselves, that helps them to make a spiritual breakthrough into God's kingdom of love.

Forbes Robinson says,

To my mind life is love, and love is life. Love is not sentimental affection, simply the readiness to die for a person. But love is the laying down of life for a person, absolutely renouncing your life for another. It means living the best life you can conceive of for the sake of one you love; knowing for certain that your life is flowing into that other person, though you may never see him again in this world. Love is purifying yourself that another may be pure. Love for one person, if it be true love, leads you at once to God, for "God is Love."[6]

Martin Buber suggests that there are no gifted or ungifted. There are only those who give of themselves or those who withhold themselves. To give love, to give in love is what we are finally called to do. It is in this way that we experience most fully what it means to be a woman. It is in this way that we transcend society's definition of us. Loving does not limit growth, but expands our ideas of self in relation to others, beyond anything that we had considered. This is where true identity lies—in the creative potential for "loving" that is in both our humanness and our response to God and His love for us.

NOTES

INTRODUCTION

1. Simone de Beauvoir, *The Second Sex* (Knopf), xiii.
2. *The New Yorker*, January 17, 1970, cartoon by O'Brian.
3. William Graham Sumner, *Folkways* (Ginn), p. 354.
4. Ibid., p. 355.
5. Simone de Beauvoir, op. cit., xxi–xxii.
6. Alma Lutz, *Susan B. Anthony* (Beacon), p. 30.
7. Ibid., p. 72.
8. Ibid., p. 310.

CHAPTER ONE

1. Simone de Beauvoir, op. cit., xxvi.
2. *Soviet Life*, March 1969, "Women, Jobs, and Family."

CHAPTER TWO

1. Jules Henry, *Culture Against Man* (Random House), pp. 84–85.
2. Betty Friedan, *The Feminine Mystique* (Dell paperback), pp. 38–39.
3. *Town and Country*, January 1970, "What's Wrong with American Women," p. 78, quote by Helen Gurley Brown.
4. *Cosmopolitan*, January 1970, "How to Be a Bitch and Make Men Like It," by W. H. Manville, p. 58.
5. Ibid., "Watch Your Dates," by Winnie Bengelsdorf, p. 34.
6. Ibid., p. 34.

CHAPTER THREE

1. Edith Hamilton, *Mythology* (Mentor), p. 70.
2. *Saturday Review*, August 8, 1970, p. 38.

CHAPTER FOUR

1. Simone de Beauvoir, op. cit., xvi.
2. Virginia Woolf, *A Room of One's Own* (Harcourt, Brace), pp. 56–57.
3. Simone de Beauvoir, op. cit., p. 711.
4. Virginia Woolf, op. cit., pp. 60–61.
5. Simone de Beauvoir, op. cit., p. xix.

CHAPTER FIVE

1. Virginia Woolf, *A Writer's Diary* (Signet), p. 59.
2. William James, *Great Books of the Western World* (William Benton), v. 53, p. 188.
3. Ibid., p. 189.
4. Watzlawick, Beavin, Jackson, *Pragmatics of Human Communication* (Norton), p. 87.
5. Rollo May, *Man's Search for Himself* (Signet), p. 112.

CHAPTER SIX

1. Paul Tournier, *A Place for You* (Harper & Row), p. 27.
2. Ibid., p. 53.
3. Eulah Laucks, Center Report, Vol. III, No. 4, p. 14.
4. Erik H. Erikson, "Reflections on Womanhood," *Daedalus*, Spring 1964, p. 588.
5. Ibid., p. 590.
6. Ibid.
7. Ibid., p. 605.
8. Robert Frost, "The Death of the Hired Man," *Quarto of American Literature* (Scribner), p. 461.

CHAPTER SEVEN

1. Elizabeth Gordon, *House Beautiful*, January 1959.

CHAPTER EIGHT

1. Rollo May, op. cit., pp. 212–13.
2. Abraham Maslow, *Toward a Psychology of Being* (Van Nostrand), p. 59.
3. George Bach and Peter Wyden, *The Intimate Enemy* (Avon), pp. 17, 18.
4. Rollo May, op. cit., p. 210.

CHAPTER TEN

1. *Redbook*, September 1970, "Sex and Marriage"—A *Redbook* discussion with Dr. William H. Masters and Mrs. Virginia Johnson, p. 89.
2. Daniel St. Albin Green, "Peoples, Societies Change Slowly," *The National Observer*, February 2, 1970, p. 20.
3. Max Coots, "For Today's Adolescents Home Is Just an Affectionate Hotel," *The National Observer*, September 7, 1970, p. 18.
4. Jules Henry, op. cit., p. 138.

CHAPTER ELEVEN

1. Thomas R. Kelly, *A Testament of Devotion* (Harper), p. 29.
2. Douglas Steere, *Rain on the Mountain* (Five Year Meetings of Friends).

CHAPTER TWELVE

1. J. H. Oldham, *Florence Allshorn* (Harper), p. 63.
2. Ibid., p. 93.
3. Erich Fromm, *The Art of Loving* (Harper), p. 26.
4. Forbes Robinson, *An Inward Legacy*, A Pendle Hill Pamphlet, No. 92, p. 8.
5. J. H. Oldham, op. cit., p. 145.
6. Forbes Robinson, op. cit., p. 11.

About the Author:

A graduate of McPherson College, Kansas, Patricia Kennedy Helman married a fellow student, A. Blair Helman who later became a minister and at thirty-five was chosen president of Manchester College in Indiana. For the past fifteen years the Helmans have lived in North Manchester, where Mrs. Helman, in addition to her full-time job as the wife of a college president, is the mother of two daughters as well as a provocative public speaker.